Mama Sita

Mama Sita's®

East - West

Cook-Book

16th Edition

Printed by:
    Progressive Printing Palace, Inc.
    120 Kamias Road
    Quezon City, Philippines
    Tel.Nos. 921-9378, 921-9381, 921-9380 & 922-2828
    Fax No. 921-9382

Illustrations by:
    Jong Vinoya, Paul Ferrer & Rex Evangelista
    Reflexions
    Evergreen Executive Vill. Phase II
    Ortigas Ave. Extension Antipolo, Rizal

A WORD FROM THE PUBLISHER

Mabuhay! It means "May you have life!"

Through this cookbook, we are happy to share with you, life-giving recipes that have been passed on from one generation to another, from one country to another.

We keep alive the teachings of our matriarch, Engracia Reyes, who was a national figure in the culinary field in our country, honored as a role model in promoting Filipino culinary arts.

We are now at the 4th generation of active clan members whose culinary expertise are still influenced by the principles our grandmother, Engracia Reyes, and her daughter, Mama Sita, lived by. They always emphasized the importance of good quality, nutritious and delicious food, the best ingredients, the most natural methods of cooking and the environment-friendly management of a kitchen .

The Mama Sita products featured in these recipes compiled by her grand daughter, Joyce, sustain their dictum of quality in every dish you cook. Their ingredients have the advantage of being organically grown with no artificial additives.

To your health and enjoyment of good food, we are dedicating this cookbook!

CLARITA REYES LAPUS
Export Champion-Processed Foods

CONTENTS

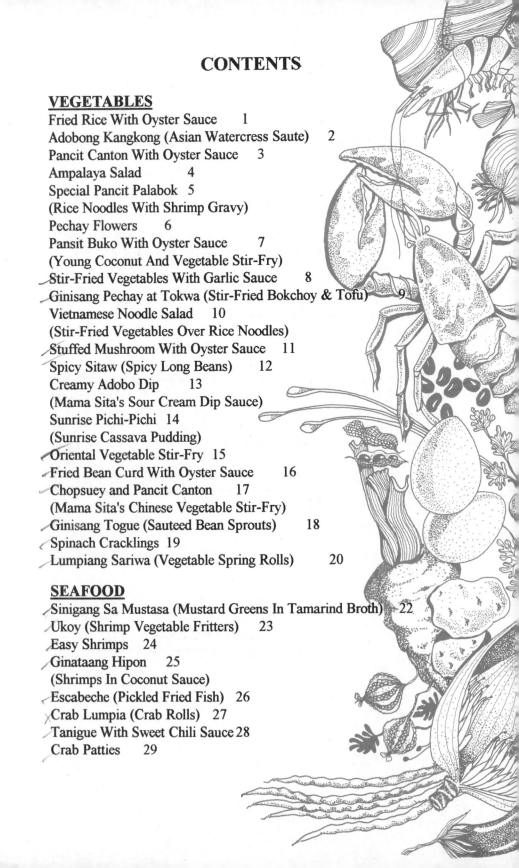

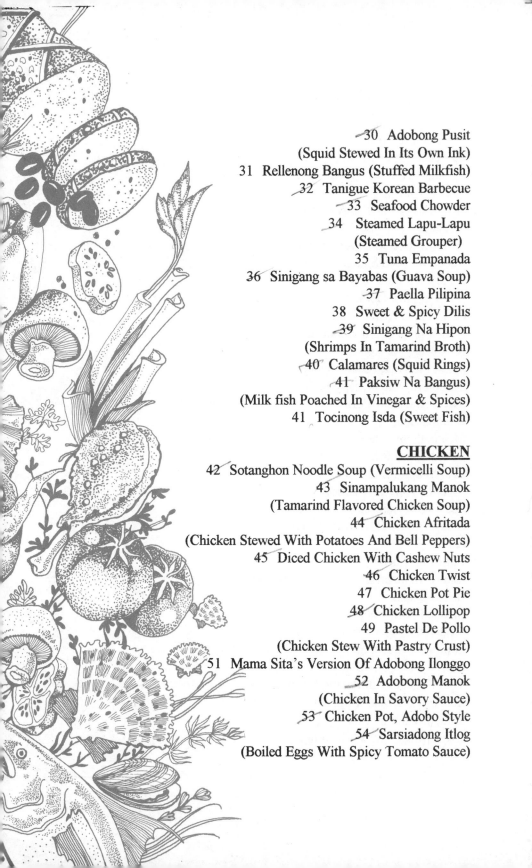

CHICKEN

MEAT

Pinsec Frito (Crispy Wontons)   55
Naiibang Lumpia   56
(Vietnamese Spring Rolls)
Barbecue   57
Longanisa (Breakfast Sausage)   58
Paksiw Na Lechon   59
(Pork Stewed In Tangy Liver Sauce)
Mechado   60
(Beef Braised In Savory Shallot Sauce)
Adobo in Coco Sauce   61
Paksiw Na Pata   62
(Pickled Pork Hocks)
Pork Asado (Sweet Pork Stew)   63
Pata Humba (Pork Hocks Stew)   64
Kare-Kare   65
(Oxtail In Rich Peanut Sauce)
Lechon Kawali (Crispy Pork)   66
Sweet And Sour Pork   67
Wonton Soup   68
Meatballs In White Sauce   70
Baked Spare Ribs   71
Beef Sinigang   72
(Beef In Tamarind Broth)
Beef With Asparagus   73
Callos (Spicy Casserole Of Tripe)   74
Fajitas 75
Chili Con Carne   77
(Spicy Mexican-Style Beef With Beans)
Baked Lechon   78
Breaded Pork Chop   79
Caldereta (Spicy Stew)   80
Lumpiang Shanghai (Chinese Spring Rolls) 81
Beef With Oyster Sauce   82
Veal Cutlets With Palabok Parfum   83
Beef or Pork With Spinach   84
Spicy Caldereta Meatballs   85
(Spicy Meatballs With Noodles)
Tocino (Sweet Pork)   86

Vegetables

*"Browsing through Mama Sita's
Fourth Generation Cookbook, one
realizes that the mix has truly
found its place in Filipino cooking."*

> Doreen Fernandez, IN GOOD TASTE
> Philippine Daily Inquirer
> April 18, 1995

*"There must be thousands of Reyeses
in this country - perhaps , even
millions - but there is only one Reyes
family associated with good cooking
and good food."*

> Rosalinda L. Orosa, TABLE TALK
> Starweek (Sunday mag. of Phil. Star)
> July 2, 1995

*"Who has not heard of Mama Sita,
or for that matter, patronized
Mama Sita's Instant food
mixes and sauces?"*

> Chona S. Trinidad, SCENE HERE,
> SEEN THERE
> The Manila Chronicle
> May 18, 1995

FRIED RICE WITH OYSTER SAUCE

**Makes 4 servings.**

			Metric		English	
3/4	tsp	**Salt**	3	g	3/28	oz
1 3/4	tsp	**Mama Sita's _Palabok_ (Shrimp Gravy) Mix**	3	g	3/28	oz
3	tbsp	**Mama Sita's Oyster Sauce**	60	g	2	oz
3	tbsp	**Cooking oil**	45	mL	1 1/2	fl oz
1 1/2	tsp	**Garlic, crushed**	5	g	3/16	oz
3	cups	**Leftover boiled rice**	400	g	14	oz
2	pcs	**Eggs, scrambled, fried and cut into strips**	120	g	4	oz
1/2	cup	**Carrots, chopped finely**	100	g	3 1/2	oz
1/2	cup	**Green peas**	85	g	3	oz

1. Dissolve salt and Mama Sita's Palabok (Shrimp Gravy) Mix in Mama Sita's Oyster Sauce.

2. Heat oil. Sauté garlic and toss in leftover boiled rice. Stir–fry over high heat until garlic is golden brown.

3. Add salt-Palabok Mix-Oyster Sauce mixture. Stir-fry.

4. Add the remaining ingredients one at a time: scrambled eggs, carrots, and green peas. Continue cooking for another 2 minutes.

Optional: You can add 1/2 cup left-over roast pork or ham cut into strips or 1 cup diced cooked shrimps.

ADOBONG KANGKONG
(Asian Watercress Sauté)

Makes 4 servings.

			Metric		English	
1	tbsp	Cooking oil	15	mL	1/2	fl oz
1	tsp	Garlic, crushed	3	g	3/28	oz
4	tbsp	Mama Sita's Barbecue Marinade	60	mL	2	fl oz
3	cups	*Kangkong* (Asian watercress) or spinach	150	g	5 1/4	oz
1	tbsp	Mama Sita's *Sukang Tuba* (Coconut Nectar Vinegar) Salt to taste	15	mL	1/2	fl oz

1. *Heat cooking oil and sauté garlic until golden brown.*

2. *Add Mama Sita's Barbecue Marinade and kangkong leaves.*

3. *When the leaves turn dark green, add the vinegar and salt.*

4. *Remove from heat and serve over hot rice.*

PANCIT CANTON WITH OYSTER SAUCE

Makes 4 servings.

			Metric		English	
2	tbsp	**Cooking oil**	30	mL	1	fl oz
2	slices	**Ginger, crushed**	5	g	1/6	oz
1 1/2	tbsp	**Garlic, crushed**	15	g	1/2	oz
1	pc	**Red Bell pepper, cut into strips**	25	g	3/4	oz
1/4	cup	**Mama Sita's Oyster Sauce**	80	g	2 3/4	oz
3/4	cup	**Water**	187	mL	6 1/3	fl oz
1	tbsp	**Soy Sauce**	15	mL	1/2	fl oz
200	g	***Pancit Canton***	200	g	7	oz
1	cup	***Chicharo* (snow peas), stringed, and blanched**	100	g	3 1/2	oz
1/2	cup	**Carrots, cut into strips and blanched**	100	g	3 1/2	oz
2	pcs	***Calamansi*, halved**	10	g	3/4	oz

1. *Heat oil in a large wok or kawali*

2. *Sauté ginger until golden.*

3. *In the same pan, add garlic and stir-fry. Add the bell pepper stir-fry for one minute.*

4. *Add the Mama Sita's Oyster Sauce dissolved in water and soy sauce and cook for 30 seconds.*

5. *Add the pancit canton and stir-fry.*

6. *As the noodles become tender, add remaining vegetables and stir-fry for one minute. Remove from heat*

7. *Serve with calamansi.*

AMPALAYA SALAD
(Bitter Gourd Salad)

Makes 4 servings.

			Metric		English	
2	cups	*Ampalaya*, sliced thinly	200	g	7	oz
2	tbsp	Rock salt	8	g	1/4	oz
3	pcs	*Sibuyas Tagalog* (shallots)	30	g	1	oz
2	pcs	Tomatoes, round thin slices	90	g	3 1/8	oz

Dressing:

4	tbsp	Mama Sita's Coconut Nectar Vinegar	60	mL	2	fl oz
4	tbsp	Water	60	mL	2	fl oz
4	tbsp	Sugar	40	g	1 1/2	oz
		dash of black pepper				

Procedure:

1. Cut ampalaya into two, lengthwise. Remove the seeds. Slice thinly crosswise.
2. Rub ampalaya slices with salt. Leave for 20 minutes.
3. Squeeze out ampalaya juice. Remove excess salt with water. Squeeze out water.
4. Cut shallots and tomatoes into thin, round slices. Chill the vegetable slices.
5. Arrange in a platter and serve with dressing.

Preparation of Dressing:

1. In a sauce pan, mix vinegar and water and let boil for 2 minutes.
2. Lower heat. Add sugar, and black pepper.
3. Stir continuously for two to three minutes. Let cool and serve with salad.

SPECIAL PANCIT PALABOK
(Noodles with Shrimp Gravy)

Makes 8 - 12 servings.

			Metric		*English*	
1/4	Kg	Pork shoulder or chicken	1/4	g	1/2	lb
3	tbsp	Cooking Oil	45	mL	1 1/2	fl oz
1	head	Garlic , crushed	20	g	3/4	oz
1/2	cup	Deboned *Tinapa*(smoked fish) flakes	30	g.	1	oz.
1	pouch	Mama Sita's *Palabok* (Shrimp Gravy) Mix	57	g	2	oz
2	cups	Soup stock (from boiling meat)	500	mL	1	pint
4	Liters	Water , and				
2	tbsp	Cooking Oil, to cook:				
1	pack	Kim's Special *Bihon* (Corn Sticks)	227	g	8	oz
2	pcs	Hard boiled eggs, sliced	2	pcs	2	pcs
2	tbsp	Garlic, fried until golden	30	g	1	oz
1/2	cup	Shrimps, boiled, shelled, and halved	100	g	3 1/2	oz
3	tbsp	*Dahon ng Sibuyas* (Spring onions) chopped	45	g	1 1/2	oz
1/2	cup	Crushed *Chicharon*	30	g	1	oz
4	pcs	*Calamansi,* sliced crosswise *Patis* (fish sauce) to taste	20	g	3/4	oz

1. Boil pork shoulder or chicken meat until tender, dice into 1/2 x 1/4 inch pieces (1 1/4 x 2/3 cm) and set aside.
2. In a wok or kawali, heat oil and sauté garlic, pork, 1/4 c. of tinapa, and stir in Mama Sita's Palabok (Shrimp Gravy) Mix dissolved in 2 cups soup stock set aside from boiling the meat. Bring to a boil while stirring constantly.
3. Lower the heat and simmer until sauce is thick. Remove from heat and set aside.
4. Cook the Kim's Special Bihon (CornSticks): Bring 4 Litres water and 2 tbsp cooking oil to a rolling boil and drop the noodles. Leave for 1 minute or until noodles are cooked. Drain and wash with cold water.
5. Arrange noodles on a bilao (bamboo tray or any round platter) lined with banana leaves. Pour sauce over and garnish with boiled egg, toasted garlic,

boiled shrimp, chopped spring onions, crushed chicharon, remaining ¼ c. of tinapa flakes, and calamansi halves .

6. *Serve with patis.*

PECHAY FLOWERS

<u>**Makes 4-6 servings.**</u>

			Metric		*English*	
1	tsp	**Salt**	4	g	1/8	oz
		White pepper to taste				
1	tsp	**Cornstarch (for shrimps)**	3	g	3/28	oz
1	tbsp	**Gin or rhum (optional)**	15	mL	1/2	fl oz
1 1/2	cups	**Shrimps (beef, pork, chicken**	1/4	Kg	9	oz
		or fish may be used)				
3	tbsp	**Cooking oil (corn or soya oil)**	45	mL	1 1/2	fl oz
1 1/2	tsp	**Ginger, minced**	10	g	1/3	oz
1	tbsp	**Garlic, minced**	10	g	1/3	oz
3	cups	***Pechay* flowers (cauliflower**	1/2	Kg	1.1	lbs
		or broccoli are good				
		substitutes)				
1	tbsp	**Mama Sita's Oyster Sauce**	20	g	3/4	oz
1	tsp	**Sugar**	4	g	1/8	oz
1	tbsp	**Soy sauce**	30	mL	1	fl oz
	1/4 cup	**Soup stock or water**	62	mL	2	fl oz
1	tsp	**Cornstarch, dissolved in**	3	g	3/28	oz
1	tbsp	**Water**	15	mL	1/2	fl oz

1. *Combine salt, white pepper, cornstarch, and gin or rhum.*
2. *Roll shrimps in cornstarch mixture. Set aside*
3. *Heat wok and add cooking oil. Sauté minced ginger and garlic.*
4. *Add shrimps and stir-fry until it turns pink.*
5. *Add vegetables, Mama Sita's Oyster Sauce, sugar, soy sauce, and soup stock or water.*
6. *Pour dissolved cornstarch to thicken.*
7. *Continue cooking over high heat until vegetables are done.*

PANSIT BUKO WITH OYSTER SAUCE
(Young Coconut and Vegetable Stir-Fry)

Makes 4 servings.

			Metric		*English*	
2	tbsp	**Cooking oil**	30	mL	2	fl oz
2	tbsp	**Garlic, crushed**	20	g	3/4	oz
1	pc	**Onion, sliced**	60	g	2	oz
1/2	cup	**Carrots, cut into strips**	100	g	3 1/2	oz
3	tbsp	**Mama Sita's Oyster Sauce**	60	g	2	oz
1	cup	**Cabbage, sliced thinly**	80	g	2 3/4	oz
2	pcs	***Buko* (young coconut), shredded**	60	g	2	oz
1	tsp	***Patis* (fish sauce)**	5	mL	1/8	fl oz
1/2	tsp	***Wansoy* or coriander leaves, for garnishing**	3	g	3/28	oz
4	pcs	***Calamansi***	20	g	3/4	oz

1. *Heat oil and sauté garlic and onion.*

2. *Add the following: carrots, Mama Sita's Oyster Sauce, cabbage, and buko.*

3. *Add the fish sauce.*

4. *Garnish with wansoy or coriander leaves.*

5. *Serve with calamansi.*

STIR-FRIED VEGETABLES WITH GARLIC SAUCE

<u>**Makes 4 servings.**</u>

			Metric		English	
1/2	cup	Carrots, sliced into thin discs	200	g	7	oz
1 1/2	cups	Button mushrooms, quartered	150	g	5 1/4	oz
2 1/3	cups	Young *chicharo* (snow peas), stringed	230	g	8 1/8	oz

Garlic Sauce:

			Metric		English	
2	tbsp	Cooking oil	30	mL	1	fl oz
3	tbsp	Garlic, minced	30	g	1	oz
1	tbsp	Ginger, minced	15	g	1/2	oz
1/4	cup	Spring onion, minced	10	g	1/3	oz

Seasoning Sauce:

			Metric		English	
1 1/2	tbsp	Cornstarch	10	g	1/3	oz
3	tbsp	Mama Sita's Oyster Sauce	60	g	2	oz
1	tsp	Sesame oil	5	mL	1/8	fl oz
1 1/2	cups	Chicken broth	375	mL	3/4	pint
		Dash of salt				

1. *Blanch the carrots, mushrooms, and chicharo separately. Set aside.*

2. *Heat cooking oil and sauté garlic, ginger, and spring onions.*

3. *Combine all the ingredients for the seasoning sauce. Mix thoroughly. Pour the seasoning sauce into the garlic sauce mixture.*

4. *Add the blanched vegetables and stir-fry until cooked.*

GINISANG PECHAY AT TOKWA
(Stir-Fried Bokchoy and Tofu)

Makes 4 servings.

			Metric		English		
1/4	cup	Cooking oil	60	mL	2		fl oz
1	pc	*Tokwa* (tofu)	100	g	3	3/4	oz
2	tsp	Garlic, crushed	10	g		1/3	oz
1	pc	Onion, sliced	45	g	1	1/2	oz
2	pcs	Ripe tomatoes, chopped	95	g	3		oz
2	tbsp	Mama Sita's Oyster Sauce	40	g	1	1/2	oz
10	bunches	*Pechay*, washed	100	g	3	3/4	oz

1. *Heat oil in a wok.*

2. *Fry tokwa until golden on all sides.*

3. *Drain tokwa and set aside. When cool, cut into 1/2 x 1/2-inch cubes.*

4. *In a same wok, sauté garlic, onion, and tomatoes.*

5. *As the tomatoes start to wilt, add tokwa and Mama Sita's Oyster Sauce.*

6. *Add pechay, stir-fry and cover. Cook on high heat until done.*

VIETNAMESE NOODLE SALAD

Makes 4 servings.

			Metric		English	
1 1/2	cups	Pork shoulder, sliced (1/3 inch thick)	1/4	Kg	9	oz
2	tbsp	Mama Sita's Barbecue Marinade	30	mL	1	fl oz
4	Liters	Water to boil:				
1/2	pack	Kim's Special _Bihon_ (Corn Sticks)	100	g	3 1/2	oz
Dressing:						
2	tbsp	Kim's Sweet Chili Sauce	30	g	1	oz
1	tbsp	Mama Sita's Premium Vinegar	15	mL	1/2	fl oz
1 1/4	tbsp	Sugar	15	g	1/2	oz
1	tsp	_Patis_ (fish sauce)	5	mL	5/28	fl oz
5	tbsp	Water	75	mL	2 1/2	fl oz
1	bundle	Native lettuce, chopped	110	g	3 3/4	oz
1	pc	Cucumber(med. size), julienned	125	g	4 1/4	oz
1/4	cup	Roasted Peanuts, chopped	45	g	1 1/2	oz
1	cup	Carrots, julienned	100	g	3 1/2	oz
26	leaves	Basil, chopped	10	g	1/3	oz

1. In a bowl, combine pork and Mama Sita's Barbecue Marinade. Marinate for 15 minutes. Grill and slice into 2 x1/2 inch pieces.

2. In a large saucepan bring 4 Liters water to a rolling boil. Blanch the bihon, rinse and set aside.

3. To make dressing: In a small bowl combine Kim's Sweet Chili Sauce, Mama Sita's Premium Vinegar, sugar, patis, and water. Mix well.

4. In a large bowl combine noodles and vegetables and the dressing.

5. Top with grilled pork slices and roasted peanuts.

Note: Leftover barbecue maybe used instead of the pork.

STUFFED MUSHROOM WITH OYSTER SAUCE

Makes 20-25 pieces.

			Metric		English	
		Water for soaking				
20-25	pcs	**Small dried mushrooms**	65	g	2 1/4	oz
1 1/2	cups	**Ground pork**	1/4	Kg	9	oz
2	pcs	**Onions, chopped finely**	120	g	4 1/4	oz
2	tbsp	**Flour**	19	g	2/3	oz
1	pc	**Egg**	60	g	2	oz
1/2	tsp	**White pepper**	2	g	1/14	oz
2	tsp	**Sesame oil**	10	mL	1/3	fl oz
1/2	tsp	**Salt**	2	g	1/14	oz
1	tbsp	**Mama Sita's Oyster Sauce**	20	g	3/4	oz

1. Soak mushrooms in plain water overnight. Cut the stems and drain.

2. Mix the remaining ingredients except the Mama Sita's Oyster Sauce.

3. Stuff mushroom with the mixture.

4. Arrange and cook in a steamer for at least 1 hour or until meat is tender.

5. Serve with a drop of Mama Sita's Oyster Sauce on top.

SPICY SITAW
(Spicy Long Beans)

Makes 4 servings.

			Metric		English	
1/4	cup	**Cooking oil**	62	mL	2	fl oz
2 1/2	cups	***Sitaw* (long beans), cut into 1" (2 1/2 cm) pieces**	1/4	Kg	9	oz
1	pc	**Onion, chopped**	60	g	2	oz
2	tbsp	**Garlic, crushed**	20	g	3/4	oz
1	pc	***Sili* (chili pepper)**	10	g	1/3	oz
2	tbsp	***Bagoong* (shrimp paste)**	12	g	1/2	oz
1	tbsp	**Gin**	15	mL	1/2	fl oz
1 1/2	cups	**Ground pork**	1/4	Kg	9	oz
2	tbsp	**Mama Sita's Barbecue Marinade**	30	mL	1	fl oz
		Sesame oil (optional)				

1. *Deep fry the sitaw, drain and set aside.*

2. *Sauté the onions, garlic, and chili pepper.*

3. *Add the shrimp paste and stir-fry. Pour in the gin.*

4. *Add the ground pork and stir-fry until cooked.*

5. *Pour in Mama Sita's Barbecue Marinade.*

6. *Add the fried sitaw. Mix well.*

7. *Just before removing from the fire, add a few drops of sesame oil.*

CREAMY ADOBO DIP
(Mama Sita's Sour Cream Dip Sauce)

For a nutritious snack for children, wash, drain, and chill fresh fruits and vegetables like sliced apples, carrots, cucumber, celery sticks or previously blanched mung bean sprouts.

Combine 1 1/2 tbsp Mama Sita's Adobo (Savory Sauce) Mix, 1 tsp sugar, and 1 cup Sour Cream (8 oz). Whip until well blended. Keep refrigerated until just before serving.

Arrange chilled vegetables attractively on a serving bowl with the dip at the center.

To make homemade Sour Cream

    1 cup   **Evaporated milk or all-purpose cream**
    1 tbsp   *Calamansi* **juice**

Mix 1 cup evaporated milk with 1 tbsp Calamansi juice. Allow the mixture to stand until it curdles and thickens.

For Light Sour Cream

Mix ingredients for 2-3 seconds in a blender.

SUNRISE PICHI-PICHI
(Sunrise Cassava Pudding)

Makes 30 pieces.

			Metric		English	
1	cup	*Cassava* (manioc)	240	g	8 1/2	oz
1	cup	**Sugar**	180	g	6 1/3	fl oz
1	cup	**Water**	240	mL	8	fl oz
1	tsp	*Lijia* (lye)	5	mL	1/6	fl oz
1	tsp	*Calamansi* or orange peel, dissolved in	5	g	1/6	oz
1	tbsp	**Water, and strained to get flavor**	15	mL	1/2	fl oz
1/2	tsp	Mama Sita's *Achuete* (Annatto) Powder	2.5	g	1/12	oz
1	cup	*Niyog* (coconut), desiccated or freshly-grated	60	g	2	oz

1. With the tip of the knife, make a small cut into the manioc. Twist tip of the knife inside the cut to remove the thick skin and expose the white flesh.

2. Cut manioc into smaller pieces to fit into the food processor. Remove the fibrons and hard core.

3. Grate until the manioc forms a smooth mass.

4. Combine grated manioc, sugar, water, lye, calamansi or orange flavoring, and Mama Sita's Achuete (Annatto) Powder and mix well.

5. Steam for 30 minutes or more until the manioc becomes translucent.

6. Remove from fire and let it cool for 15 minutes.

7. Scoop 1 tbsp (20 g) of the cooked mixture, form into a ball, and roll in freshly grated coconut. (If unavailable, use desiccated coconut.)

8. Arrange on a platter and serve with pandan tea or salabat (ginger brew).

ORIENTAL VEGETABLE STIR-FRY

			Metric		*English*	
2	tbsp	Cooking oil for sautéing	30	mL	2	fl oz
1	tbsp	Ginger, crushed	10	g	1/3	oz
1	tbsp	Garlic, crushed	10	g	1/3	oz
1	cup	Mushrooms (Shitake or button), quartered	120	g	4 1/4	oz
2	cups	Asparagus or broccoli, cut into pieces and blanched or steamed	200	g	7	oz
3	tbsp	Mama Sita's Oyster Sauce	60	g	2 1/8	oz
1	tbsp	Cornstarch, dissolved in:	7	g	1/4	oz
1/4	cup	Water	63	mL	2 1/8	fl oz
1	pack	Soft tofu, sliced 1/2" inch thick	250	g	1/2	lb

1. *Heat oil in a wok and sauté ginger.*

2. *Add garlic and sauté, taking care not to brown the garlic.*

3. *Increase the heat, add mushrooms, and sauté for another 3 minutes or until mushrooms are cooked. (Be careful not to over cook or the mushrooms will shrink.)*

4. *Add asparagus or broccoli, and Mama Sita's Oyster Sauce, stir-fry for another 30 seconds.*

5. *Taste the sauce and add salt or soy sauce as needed.*

6. *Add cornstarch and water, lower the heat and simmer until sauce thickens.*

7. *Add soft tofu and cook for another 30 seconds.*

FRIED BEAN CURD WITH OYSTER SAUCE

Makes 4 servings.

			Metric		English	
4	tbsp	**Cooking oil**	60	mL	2	fl oz
5	pcs	_Tokwa_ **(tofu), cubed (1/2 x 1/2 inch) thick**		1/2 Kg	9	oz
1	cup	**Fresh button mushrooms, washed and sliced**	120	g	4 1/4	oz
3	tbsp	**Mama Sita's Oyster Sauce Dash of black pepper**	60	g	2	oz
1/4	cup	**Spring onions, sliced into 1/2" (1 cm) pieces**	20	g	3/4	oz

1. _Heat the oil and fry the tokwa until it starts to form a golden brown crust. Remove the tokwa from the pan and set aside._

2. _In the same pan, stir-fry the mushrooms for 3 to 5 minutes._

3. _Add the Mama Sita's Oyster Sauce, fried tokwa and black pepper. Mix well and cook for another 2 minutes._

4. _When the mushrooms start to wilt, add the spring onions and remove from heat._

5. _Serve immediately._

CHOPSUEY and PANCIT CANTON
(Mama Sita's Chinese Vegetable Stir-fry)

Makes 4-6 servings.

			Metric		English	
1	pouch	Mama Sita's *Pancit Canton/* *Chopsuey* (Stir-Fry) Mix	40	g	1 1/2	oz
1	cup	Water	250	mL	8 1/2	fl oz
3	tbsp	Cooking oil	45	mL	1 1/2	fl oz
1 1/3	cups	Meat, sliced thinly or shrimps, shelled and deveined	230	g	8 1/8	oz
3	cups	Assorted vegetables, sliced (carrots, celery, cauliflower, cabbage, snowpeas, mushrooms, etc.)	1/2 Kg		1.1	lbs
1	tsp	Mama Sita's Oyster Sauce (optional)	7	g	1/4	oz
1	tsp	Sesame oil (optional)	5	mL	1/8	fl oz

1. Dissolve Mama Sita's Pancit Canton/Chopsuey (Stir-Fry) Mix in water. Set aside.

2. In a pan with cooking oil fry meat or shrimp quickly over high heat.

3. Add assorted vegetables.

4. Stir in dissolved mix. Add Mama Sita's Oyster Sauce and sesame oil. Cook, for 3 minutes.

5. Serve hot.

For Pancit Canton:

Plunge 8 1/8 oz (230 g) canton noodles into 6 cups (1 1/2 L) boiling water. Separate noodles with fork while cooking for 1 minute. Drain in a colander. Let dry by arranging noodles with a fork on a tray. Set aside. Prepare chopsuey and stir in cooked noodles just before removing from fire.

GINISANG TOGUE
(Sautéed Bean Sprouts)

Makes 6 servings.

			Metric		English	
2	tbsp	Cooking oil for sautéing	30	mL	2	fl oz
2	pcs	*Tokwa* (tofu), approximately 1/2x1/2 inch cubed	120	g	4 1/4	oz
2	tbsp	Garlic, crushed	20	g	3/4	oz
1	pc	Onion, sliced	60	g	2	oz
2	pcs	Tomatoes, sliced	90	g	3 1/8	oz
9	cups	*Togue* (mung bean sprout), washed and drained	1/4	Kg	9	oz
2	tbsp	Mama Sita's Oyster Sauce	20	g	3/4	oz
1/4	tsp	Black pepper	1	g	1/28	oz
1/4	tsp	Salt	1	g	1/28	oz
2	tsp	*Patis* (fish sauce)	5	mL	1/8	fl oz

1. *In a wok, heat some oil and fry tokwa until golden on all sides. Set aside and dice into 1/2 x 1/2-inch cubes.*

2. *In the same wok, sauté garlic, onion, and tomatoes.*

3. *As the tomatoes start to wilt, add the tokwa, bean sprouts, Mama Sita's Oyster Sauce, patis, salt, and black pepper.*

4. *Continue cooking over medium heat until bean sprouts are done.*

SPINACH CRACKLINGS

Approximately 55 cracklings (1 1/2 - 3 inches each).

			Metric		*English*		
1	bundle	**Spinach**	265	g	9	1/3	oz
1/4	cup	**Flour**	30	g	1		oz
1/4	cup	**Cornstarch**	25	g		3/4	oz
1/4	cup and						
2	tbsp	**Water**	78	mL	2	2/3	fl oz
		Salt, dash					
		Pepper, dash					
		Cooking oil for deep frying					

1. *Remove spinach leaves from stems and rinse thoroughly.*

2. *In a bowl, combine flour, cornstarch, salt, and pepper.*

3. *Gradually mix in the water and stir until well blended.*

4. *In a deep fryer or small saucepan, heat enough oil fill the pan 2 inches deep.*

5. *Dip a leaf in the batter and deep fry.*

6. *Before it turns golden remove and drain on paper towels.*

7. *Repeat for remaining leaves, taking care not to overcrowd the pan.*

8. *Serve with Mama Sita's Coconut Nectar Vinegar or Mama Sita's Adobo Dip (see page 13.)*

LUMPIANG SARIWA
(Vegetable Spring Rolls)

Makes 10-12 rolls.

Metric   *English*

Filling:

			Metric		English	
1/4	cup	Cooking oil	60	mL	2	fl oz
3/4	cup	Sweet potato, diced (1/2" x 1/2")	100	g	3 1/2	oz
1	tbsp	Garlic, crushed	10	g	1/3	oz
1/2	pc	Onion, sliced	30	g	1	oz
1/4	tsp	Mama Sita's *Achuete* (Annatto) Powder	1	g	1/28	oz
1	cup	Green beans, blanched and diced	150	g	5 1/4	oz
2 1/2	cups	Bean sprouts, rinsed	200	g	7	oz
1	tbsp	Mama Sita's Oyster Sauce Dash of white pepper Salt to taste	20	g	3/4	oz

Wrapper:

1	cup	Flour	150	g	5 1/4	oz
1/2	cup	Cornstarch	60	g	2	oz
1 1/2	cup	Water	375	mL	12 2/3	fl oz
2	pcs	Eggs	120	g	4	oz
3	tbsp	Cooking oil	45	mL	2 1/2	fl oz

Sauce:

6	tbsp	Cornstarch	45	g	1 1/2	oz
1/2	cup	Sugar	80	g	2 3/4	oz
2	cups	Water	500	mL	17	fl oz
4	tbsp	Soy Sauce	60	mL	2	fl oz
2	tbsp	Toasted Peanuts, chopped	20	g	3/4	oz
1	tbsp	Garlic, crushed	15	g	1/2	oz

1. *In a pan, fry sweet potatoes until tender.*
2. *In the same pan, sauté garlic and onion until onion starts to wilt. Add the Mama Sita's Achuete (Annatto) Powder and stir-fry.*
3. *Add the green beans, sweet potato, bean sprouts and Mama Sita's Oyster Sauce. Stir-fry until cooked. Set aside.*

4. **Wrapper**: *In a bowl, combine all dry ingredients and make a well in the center, gradually mix in egg, water and oil. Stir until it forms a smooth batter. Pour onto a heated 6-inch Teflon pan, approximately 1/4 cup at a time.*
5. **Sauce**: *In a small pan, combine sugar, cornstarch, water, and soy sauce, stir over medium heat until thick.*
6. *Line the wrapper with a curly lettuce leaf and place 2-3 tbsp of filling on it. Roll and seal. Serve with brown sauce, chopped garlic and toasted peanuts.*

SINIGANG SA MUSTASA
(Mustard Greens In Tamarind Broth)

Makes 6 servings.

			Metric		_English_	
1	tbsp	**Garlic**	10	g	1/3	oz
1/4	cup	**Cooking oil**	60	mL	2	fl oz
2 1/2	tsp	**Ginger, crushed**	12.5	g	1/3	oz
2	pcs	**Onion, sliced**	80	g	2 3/4	oz
3	pcs	**Tomatoes, chopped**	95	g	3 1/3	oz
1	pc	_Labanos_ **(radish), peeled and** cut diagonally	120	g	4 1/4	oz
1	cup	_Okra_**, sliced**	150	g	5 1/4	oz
1	bundle	_Mustasa_ **(Mustard Greens)**	125	g	4 1/3	oz
3	pcs	_Sili_ **(green chili pepper), sliced** into two	30	g	1	oz
5	cups	**Water**	1 1/4	L	2 1/2	pints
1	pouch	**Mama Sita's** _Sinigang_ **(Tamarind Seasoning) Mix**	25	g	1	oz
10 - 12	pcs	_Sugpo_ **(prawns), trimmed**	1/4	Kg	9	oz
1/2	tbsp	_Patis_ **(fish sauce)**	7	mL	1/4	fl oz

1. _In a sauce pan heat oil. Sauté ginger, garlic, onion, and tomatoes._

2. _Add the vegetables (labanos, okra, mustasa and sili) and stir fry._

3. _Remove the mustasa and set aside. Add 5 cups of water and Mama Sita's Sinigang (Tamarind Seasoning) Mix. Continue to simmer for 3 minutes._

4. _Add the prawns and simmer for another 3 minutes. Add the patis and stir._

5. _Turn off the heat and add the mustasa._

6. _Serve immediately._

Seafoods

"I started with a Sinigang na Hipon...
It was full of flavor and had kangkong,
whole green chilis and Chinese radish.
The sourish taste was not overpowering,
it was tangy and whetted the appetite.

On the whole, meal at $12.50
per person, was a taste-opener"

Khng Eu Meng
The Strait Times, Singapore
November 19, 1987

UKOY
(Shrimp -Vegetable Fritters)

Makes about one dozen 2" fritters.

Batter:

			Metric		English	
1/2	cup	All-purpose flour	75	g	2 2/3	oz
1/2	cup	Cornstarch	60	g	2	oz
1/3	cup	Mama Sita's *Palabok* (Shrimp Gravy) Mix	50	g	1 3/4	oz
3/4	cup	Water, cold	187	mL	6 1/3	fl oz
1	cup	*Kalabasa* (squash), shredded	150	g	5 1/4	oz
1/2	cup	Carrots, shredded	100	g	3 1/2	oz
1/4	cup	Leeks, minced	25	g	1	oz
1	pc	*Tokwa* (tofu), cut into 1/2" cubes	60	g	2	oz
12	pcs	Shrimps, small, peeled and deveined (optional) Cooking oil for frying	1/4	Kg	9	oz

Garlic Dipping Sauce:

1/2	cup	Mama Sita's Coconut Nectar Vinegar	125	mL	4 1/4	fl oz
2	tsp	Garlic, crushed Dash of black pepper Pinch of salt	20	g	3/4	oz

1. **To prepare the Batter:**
   In a mixing bowl, combine all-purpose flour, cornstarch, Mama Sita's Palabok (Shrimp Gravy) Mix, and water. Stir in squash, carrots, and leeks.
2. **To form the fritters:**
   In a saucer, form batter mixture into small 2" patties. Top with a shrimp and 3 tofu cubes. Gently slide into pre-heated pan with 350°F (170°C) cooking oil and fry until golden brown, about 5 minutes. Drain off excess oil. Continue process until you use up the batter mixture.
   Serve hot with garlic dipping sauce.
3. **To prepare the Garlic Dip:**
   In a bowl, combine vinegar, garlic, black pepper, and salt. Stir.
   Let stand for at least 20 minutes. Reserve until needed.

23

EASY SHRIMPS

			Metric		English	
6	cups	**Shrimps**	1	Kg	2.2	lbs
1/2	cup	**Mama Sita's Barbecue Marinade**	125	mL	4 1/4	fl oz
2	tbsp	**Cooking oil**	30	mL	1	fl oz

1. *Marinate shrimps in Mama Sita's Barbecue Marinade for 30 minutes.*

2. *Drain and reserve marinade.*

3. *Stir-fry shrimps in hot oil.*

4. *Add the reserved Mama Sita's Barbecue Marinade.*

5. *When the sauce starts to boil, remove from heat.*

6. *Serve hot.*

GINATAANG HIPON
(Shrimps in Coconut Sauce)

Makes 4-6 servings:

			Metric		English	
2	tbsp	Cooking oil	30	mL	1	fl oz
1	tbsp	Garlic, crushed	10	g	1/3	oz
1	pc	Onion, sliced	60	g	2	oz
2 1/2	cups	Coconut milk	625	mL	1 1/4	pints
2	pcs	Long green pepper	20	g	3/4	oz
6	cups	Prawns, marinated for 15 minutes in :	1	Kg	2.2	lbs
1	pouch	Mama Sita's *Caldereta* (Spicy Sauce) Mix	50	g	1 3/4	oz

1. *Remove head and shell of prawns. Leave tails on. Set aside head and shell.*

2. *Sauté garlic and onion in cooking oil.*

3. *Add coconut milk and green pepper.*

4. *When it starts bubbling, add marinated shrimps.*

5. *Stir-fry until shrimps change in color.*

6. *Serve with rice or over deep fried bihon (rice noodles).*

ESCABECHE
(Pickled Fried Fish)

Makes 4 servings.

			Metric		English	
3	tbsp	Cooking oil	45	mL	2 1/2	fl oz
1	tsp	Garlic, crushed	3	g	3/28	oz
2	pcs	Onion, sliced	120	g	4 1/4	oz
1	tbsp	Ginger, sliced thinly	20	g	3/4	oz
8	pcs	Peppercorn, whole	1	g	1/28	oz
1/4	cup	Carrot, sliced into discs	50	g	1 3/4	oz
1	pc	Bell pepper, cubed (optional)	50	g	1 3/4	oz
1	pouch	Mama Sita's Sweet & Sour Sauce Mix, dissolved in	57	g	2	oz
1/2	cup	Water	125	mL	4 1/4	fl oz
3	pcs	Fried whole fish or fish fillets (lapu-lapu *(grouper)* is ideal)	1/2	Kg	1.1	lbs

1. Sauté garlic, onion, ginger, peppercorns, carrots, and bell pepper in cooking oil until half-cooked.

2. Pour in the dissolved Mama Sita's Sweet & Sour Sauce Mix.

3. Stir until thick (about 5 minutes).

4. Add the fish and simmer for 2 minutes.

5. Serve hot.

CRAB LUMPIA
(Crab Rolls)

Makes 4 servings or 20 rolls.

Filling:

			Metric		English	
1 1/2	cups	**Crabmeat**	1/4 Kg		9	oz
2	tbsp	***Dahon ng Sibuyas* (Spring onion), chopped finely**	4	g	1/8	oz
2	tbsp	**Mama Sita's Barbecue Marinade Mix**	30	g	1	oz
1/2	tsp	**Salt**	2	g	1/14	oz
1	pc	**Egg, beaten**	60	g	2	oz
1	pc	**Onion, chopped finely**	60	g	2	oz
2	tbsp	**Cornstarch**	14	g	1/2	oz
1	tsp	**Sesame oil**	5	mL	1/8	fl oz
20	pcs	**Lumpia (spring roll) pastry wrapper** **Cooking oil, for deep frying**	(12cm. dm.)		(4 3/4" dm.)	

Dipping Sauce:

			Metric		English	
1	pouch	**Mama Sita's Sweet & Sour Sauce Mix, dissolved in**	57	g	2	oz
3/4	cup	**Water**	187	mL	6 1/3	fl oz

1. *Combine filling ingredients and mix thoroughly. Chill for 30 minutes.*

2. *Spoon 1 tbsp of the mixture onto the lumpia wrapper.*

3. *Brush the edges with eggwhites or water and roll tightly to seal.*

4. *In a wok, heat enough oil for deep-frying. When hot enough, drop the crab rolls one by one and fry until golden brown.*

5. *Serve with Dipping Sauce*

TANIGUE WITH SWEET CHILI SAUCE
(King Fish with Sweet Chili Sauce)

Makes 2 servings.

			Metric		English	
2	pcs	*Tanigue* steaks, (cut into 1/4" thick)	1/4	Kg	9	oz
1	pc	*Calamansi*	5	g	1/6	oz
1/4	cup	Cooking oil	60	mL	2	fl oz
3/4	cup	Kim's Sweet Chili Sauce	186	mL	7 1/2	fl oz
1/2	pc	Carrots, sliced thinly	50	g	1 3/4	oz

1. Rub tanigue steaks with calamansi. Set aside.

2. Heat the oil in a skillet or flat frying pan.

3. Fry tanigue steaks taking care not to overcrowd the pan.

4. Pour in the Kim's Sweet Chili Sauce and carrots. Simmer for a few minutes, and remove from heat as soon as carrots are cooked.

5. Serve hot.

CRAB PATTIES

**Makes 15 pieces (approximately 1 1/2 inches in diameter).**

			Metric		English	
1 1/2	cups	**Crab meat**	1/4	Kg	1/2	lb
1 1/4	tbsp	**Mama Sita's Barbecue Marinade Mix**	12	g	1/2	oz
3	pcs	**Spring onion, chopped**	4	g	1/8	oz
1	pc	**Onion, chopped finely**	1/2	Kg	1.1	lbs
1	pc	**Egg**	60	g	2 1/8	oz
1	pc	**Bread, chopped finely and soaked in:**	25	g	2 1/2	oz
1	pc	**Egg, beaten**	60	g	2 1/8	oz
1	tbsp	**Celery, chopped finely**	25	g	2 1/2	oz
2	tbsp	**Cornstarch**	15	g	1/2	oz
1	cup	**Cooking oil**	250	mL	8 1/2	fl oz

1. Combine all ingredients and mix thoroughly except cooking oil. Chill for 30 minutes.

2. Form the mixture into patties about 1 1/2 inch in diameter (or 25g each).

3. In a wok, heat enough oil for deep-frying. Drop the patties and fry one by one until golden brown.

4. Serve with Mama Sita's Sweet & Sour Sauce or Kim's Sweet Chili Sauce.

ADOBONG PUSIT
(Squid Stewed in its own Ink)

Makes 4 servings.

			Metric		English	
6	pcs	**Squid, medium-sized, cleaned, remove inkbag and dilute in:**	1/2	Kg	1.1	lbs
1/2	cup	**Water**	250	mL	2	fl oz
3	tbsp	**Mama Sita's Coconut Nectar Vinegar**	45	mL	1 1/2	fl oz
2	tbsp	**Cooking oil**	30	mL	1	fl oz
1	tbsp	**Garlic, crushed**	10	g	1/3	oz
1	tsp	**Ginger, chopped**	7	g	1/4	oz
1	pc	**Onion, coarsely chopped**	60	g	2	oz
3	pcs	**Tomatoes**	190	g	6 3/4	oz
2	tbsp	**Mama Sita's Oyster Sauce**	40	g	1 1/2	oz
1	tsp	**Sugar**	1	g	1/28	oz
1/4	tsp	**Salt**	1	g	1/28	oz
2	tbsp	_**Kutsay**_**, minced**	4	g	1/8	oz
		Dash of ground black pepper				

1. _In a small saucepan, combine the squid, Mama Sita's Coconut Vinegar, and water. Bring to a boil and simmer until tender._

2. _Sauté·ginger, garlic, onion, and tomatoes in cooking oil. As the tomatoes start to wilt, add the squid mixture and stir-fry._

3. _Pour in the rest of the ingredients and simmer for 5 minutes._

4. _Serve hot with rice._

RELLENONG BANGUS
(Stuffed Milkfish)

Makes 4-6 servings.

			Metric		English	
2	pcs	**Whole *Bangus* (milkfish)**	1	Kg	2.2	lbs
1/4	cup	**Mama Sita's Oyster Sauce**	80	g	2 3/4	oz
1	tbsp	***Calamansi* (lemon) juice**	15	mL	1/2	fl oz
1	cup	**Water**	250	mL	8 1/2	fl oz
2	tbsp	**Cooking oil, for sautéing**	30	mL	1	fl oz
2/3	cup	**Onion, chopped finely**	80	g	2 3/4	oz
1/2	cup	**Carrots, chopped finely**	100	g	3 1/2	oz
1	pc	**Potato, chopped finely**	100	g	3 1/2	oz
1/2	cup	**Green peas**	75	g	2 2/3	oz
1/3	cup	**Raisins**	40	g	1 1/2	oz
2	pcs	**Eggs, beaten**	120	g	4 1/4	oz
2	cups	**Cooking oil, for deep frying**	500	mL	1	pint

1. *Clean and scale the fish. Place the fish on a flat surface. Pound the body with the back of a knife or a mallet. Press your left hand firmly against the fish and with your right hand, jerk the tail upward. The idea is to break the middle bone of the fish. With a spoon, scrape out all the flesh and set it aside. Discard the middle bone.*

2. *Combine the Mama Sita's Oyster Sauce with the calamansi juice. Marinate the fish skin in this mixture for 30 minutes. Set aside the marinade.*

3. *In a medium-sized saucepan, boil water; add the fish meat, cooking just until it turns white. Drain and pick out the bones.*

4. *In a wok, heat oil and sauté the onions. Add the carrots, potatoes, and green peas. Stir-fry.*

5. *When the vegetables are tender, add the fish meat, marinade, and raisins.*

6. *Remove from heat and add the beaten eggs.*

7. *Stuff this mixture into the fish skin until it reaches the neck. Deep fry with its head intact until the fish is golden brown.*

Variation: Wrap in banana leaf or aluminum foil and bake at 325°F for 45 minutes.

TANIGUE KOREAN BARBECUE
(King Fish Korean Barbecue)

<u>**Makes 2 servings.**</u>

			Metric		English	
1	tbsp	**Spring onion**	7	g	1/4	oz
1/2	tbsp	**Sesame seeds, toasted**	5	g	1/8	oz
2	tbsp	**Mama Sita's Barbecue Marinade**	30	mL 1		fl oz
1	tsp	**Sesame oil**	5	mL	1/8	fl oz
2	pcs	***Tanigue* steaks**	1/4	Kg	1/2	lb

Sauce:

1	tbsp	**Mama Sita's Barbecue Marinade**	15	mL	1/2	fl oz
1 1/2	tsp	**Spring onion, chopped**	2	stalks	2	stalks
1	tsp	**Sesame seeds, toasted**	5	g	1/8	oz
1/2	tsp	**Sesame oil**	3	mL	3/28	fl oz

1. *Combine spring onion, sesame oil, sesame seeds, and Mama Sita's Barbecue Marinade.*

2. *In a shallow pan, marinate tanigue for 30 minutes.*

3. *Heat some oil in a skillet or flat frying pan. Fry tanigue steaks taking care not to overcrowd the pan.*

4. *Combine all ingredients for the sauce and drizzle on the tanigue steaks.*

5. *Serve immediately.*

SEAFOOD CHOWDER

Makes 4 servings.

			Metric		English	
		Water to soak clams				
3	cups	*Halaan* (clams)	1/2	Kg	1.1	lbs
2	cups	**Water (for clam stock)**	500	mL	1	pint
2	tbsp	**Cooking oil**	30	mL	1	fl oz
1	pc	**Onion, chopped finely**	60	g	2	oz
2	tbsp	**Leeks, chopped finely**	15	g	1/2	oz
2/3	cup	**Carrots, diced**	130	g	4 1/2	oz
2	pc	*Laurel* (Bay) leaves	1	g	1/28	oz
1	tbsp	**Garlic, chopped finely**	10	g	1/3	oz
3/4	cup	**Fresh milk**	187	mL	6 1/3	fl oz
1/4	cup	**Mama Sita's *Palabok***	57	g	2	oz
		(Shrimp Gravy) Mix				
1	tsp	**Grated orange rind (optional)**	3	g	3/28	oz

1. *Soak the clams in water for several hours to remove the sand. Drain clams carefully.*

2. *Place clams in saucepan and add enough water to cover. Let it boil.*

3. *When the clams open, turn off the heat. (Do not use unopened shells.)*

4. *Set aside 1 1/2 cup (375 mL.) of the clam stock and discard the rest.*

5. *Heat oil. Sauté onions, leeks, and carrots. Add bay leaves.*

6. *Add the clam stock, garlic, milk, and Mama Sita's Palabok (Shrimp Gravy) Mix.*

7. *Continue stirring until the soup starts to thicken.*

8. *Add the clams and grated orange rind.*

9. *Simmer for another 2 minutes. Serve with slices of French bread and some garlic-flavored mayonnaise.*

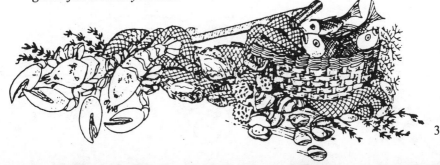

STEAMED LAPU-LAPU
(Steamed Grouper)

Makes 6 servings.

			Metric		English	
2	pcs	medium-sized *Lapu-lapu*, (Grouper) trimmed	1	Kg	2.2	lbs
3/4	cup	Ginger, sliced	240	g	8 1/2	oz
1	tsp	Rock salt	4	g	1/7	oz
2	tbsp	Cooking oil	30	mL	1	fl oz
2	tbsp	Garlic	20	g	3/4	oz
2	tbsp	Ginger, cut into strips	40	g	1 1/2	oz
1/2	cup	Mama Sita's Barbecue Marinade	125	mL	4 1/4	fl oz
1/4	cup	Mama Sita's Oyster Sauce	80	g	2 3/4	fl oz
2	tbsp	Brown sugar	20	g	3/4	oz
2	tbsp	Soy sauce	30	mL	1	fl oz
1/4	cup	Water	62	mL	2	fl oz
		Few drops of sesame oil				
1	tbsp	*Wansoy* (cilantro or coriander)	18	g	2/3	oz

1. *Fill the fish stomach with ginger slices and rub the skin with salt.*

2. *Steam or bake the fish until cooked.*

3. *Heat oil. Fry the garlic until golden brown and set aside.*

4. *Fry the ginger until crispy and set aside.*

5. *Combine Mama Sita's Barbecue Marinade, Mama Sita's Oyster Sauce, brown sugar, soy sauce, water, and the cooking oil used in frying the garlic and ginger. Simmer over medium heat until the sugar has dissolved.*

6. *Add sesame oil.*

7. *Place the steamed fish on a platter; pour the sauce over it and top with fried ginger, garlic, and wansoy leaves.*

TUNA EMPANADA

Makes 26 pieces.
Filling:

			Metric		_English_	
2	tbsp	**Cooking oil**	30	mL	1	fl oz
2	tbsp	**Garlic, minced**	10	g	1/3	oz
1	pc	**Onion, diced**	30	g	1	oz
2	cans	**Tuna, flaked**	185	g	6 1/2	oz
1	pouch	**Mama Sita's _Menudo_**	30	g	1	oz
		Afritada **(Meat Stew)Mix**				
		dissolved in:				
1	cup	**Water**	250	mL	8 1/2	fl oz
1	cup	**Potatoes, diced (1/2"x1/2")**	170	g	6	oz
1/4	cup	**Raisins**	30	g	1	oz

Crust:

2 1/2	cups	**Flour**	375	g	13 1/3	oz
1	tsp	**Salt**	4	g	1/8	oz
1	tbsp	**Sugar**	10	g	1/3	oz
12	tbsp	**Shortening**	130	g	5	oz
8	tbsp	**Ice cold water**	63	mL	2 1/8	fl oz

1. _In a pan heat oil, sauté garlic and onion for 2 minutes._
2. _Add tuna flakes, sauté for 2 minutes._
3. _Add the dissolved Mama Sita's Menudo Afritada (Meat Stew) Mix and potatoes. Simmer until sauce thickens._
4. _Add the raisins and simmer for 2 minutes._

Crust:
1. _In a large bowl, combine flour, salt, and sugar together._
2. _Add the shortening to flour mixture and cut it with a pastry blender until sandy._
3. _Add water one tbsp at a time to form into ball. Roll out the dough and cut into 1 ½" round pieces._

To assemble the Empanada:
Place 1 teaspoonful of the prepared filling at the center of each piece of crust. Fold it forming half moon shape pieces. Twist the edges to seal completely. Arrange them on cookie sheet and brush top with eggwash. Bake at 350°F for about 30 minutes.

Note: Tuna can be substituted with pork or boiled chicken.

SINIGANG SA BAYABAS
(Guava Soup)

Makes 4 servings.

			Metric		English	
3	cups	**Water**	750	mL	1 1/2	pints
1	pouch	**Mama Sita's** _Sinigang sa Bayabas_				
		(Guava Soup Base) Mix	40	g	1 1/2	oz.
1	pc	_Bangus_ **or trout, scaled and**				
		sliced diagonally	1/2	Kg	1.1	lbs.
2	cups	_Sitaw_ **(long beans), cut in 2"**				
		lengths	200	g	7	oz.
2	pcs	**Long green pepper**	20	g		3/4 oz.
1	bundle	_Kangkong_ **(swamp cabbage)**	100	g	3	1/2 oz.
		Salt to taste				
		patis (fish sauce) to taste				

1. _Boil 3 cups of water. Add Mama Sita's Sinigang sa Bayabas (Guava Soup Base) Mix and stir to dissolve. Simmer._

2. _Add fish. Cover, let boil, then simmer for 10 minutes._

3. _Add long beans and long green pepper. When almost cooked, add swamp cabbage. Simmer for two to three minutes. Add salt or fish sauce to taste. Serve with rice._

PAELLA PILIPINA

Makes 8 servings.

			Metric		English	
1	cup	_Malagkit_ (glutinous rice)	1/4 Kg		9	oz
1 1/2	cups	Long grain rice	350	g	12 1/3	oz
5	cups	Chicken stock	1 1/4 L		2 1/2	pints
1	tsp	Mama Sita's _Achuete_ (Annatto) Powder	3	g	3/28	oz
2	tbsp	Olive oil or vegetable oil	30	mL	1	fl oz
1	pc	_Chorizo_ (Spanish sausage), cut into 1/2" diagonal slices	100	g	3 1/2	oz
1 1/3	cups	Shrimps, peeled and deveined	230	g	8 1/8	oz
7	pcs	Squid, small, cut into 1/4" diagonal rings	230	g	8 1/8	oz
1	tsp	Garlic, minced	3	g	3/28	oz
1/2	cup	Onions, chopped	60	g	2	oz
2	pcs	Tomatoes, medium-sized, cored, seeded, and chopped	90	g	3 1/8	oz
1	pc	Red bell pepper, medium-sized, cored, seeded, and minced	50	g	1 3/4	oz
1	tbsp	_Patis_ (fish sauce)	15	mL	1/2	fl oz
3	tbsp	Mama Sita's _Caldereta_ (Spicy Sauce) Mix	30	g	1	oz
2	pcs	Blue crabs, medium-sized, split in halves	1/4 Kg		9	oz
1 1/3	cups	_Tahong_ (mussels), beards removed	230	g	8 1/8	oz
1 1/3	cups	_Halaan_ (clams), soaked in water for 30 minutes to remove sand	230	g	8 1/8	oz
1	pc	Red bell pepper, medium-sized, cored, seeded, and cut into strips	50	g	1 3/4	oz
1	pc	Green bell pepper, medium.-sized, cored, seeded, and cut into strips	50	g	1 3/4	oz
2/3	cup	Green peas	100	g	3 1/2	oz
1	pc	Hard boiled egg, cut into thin round slices (optional)	60	g	2	oz
2	tbsp	_Dahon ng sibuyas_ (spring onions), chopped for garnish	4	g	1/8	oz

1. *In a pot, combine the glutinous and long grain rice. Rinse twice. Drain. Add 4 1/2 cup (1.2 L) chicken stock and Mama Sita's Achuete (Annatto) Powder. Stir until well blended. Bring to a boil, lower the heat, and simmer. Cover and cook until done, about 20 minutes. Turn off heat and allow to cool for at least 10 minutes. Set aside.*
2. *In a paellera or a large sauté pan, heat oil. Sauté chorizo for 1 minute. Reserve. Sauté shrimp for about 2-3 minutes. Reserve. Add squid, sauté for 1 minute or just until it changes color to a milky white. Reserve.*
3. *In the same pan, over high heat, sauté garlic and onion for 30 seconds. Add tomatoes and minced red pepper. Sauté for 1 minute.*
4. *Add fish sauce, the remaining 1/2 cup (125 mL) stock and Mama Sita's Caldereta (Spicy Sauce) Mix. Bring mixture to a boil, lower the heat, and arrange crabs on top. Cover and simmer for 5 minutes.*
5. *Add mussels and clams. Continue to simmer for another 3 minutes or until shells open. Remove cover.*
6. *Stir in red and green bell pepper strips and peas. Cook the mixture for another minute.*
7. *To finish, add the Annatto rice, chorizo, shrimp, and squid. Toss until the mixture is well blended.*
8. *Garnish top with boiled egg and spring onions, if desired. Serve hot.*

SWEET & SPICY DILIS

Makes 4-6 servings.

			Metric		English	
2	tbsp	**Cooking oil**	30	mL	1	fl oz
1 1/2	cups	***Dilis***	60	g	2	oz
1/4	cup	**Sugar plus**				
2	tbsp	**Sugar**	85	g	3	oz
1	tsp	**Mama Sita's *Sinigang* (Tamarind Seasoning) Mix**	4	g	2/28	oz
2	pcs	**Chili, chopped**				

1. *In a frying pan heat oil.*
2. *Add dilis and stir-fry for 3 minutes or until dilis become crispy.*
3. *In another pan (preferably one with a thick bottom) caramelize the sugar.*
4. *When sugar turns golden, turn off the heat.*
5. *Add the Mama Sita's Sinigang (Tamarind Seasoning)Mix and chili pepper. Stir.*
6. *Quickly add dilis and mix well.*
7. *Transfer to a tray and cool.*

SINIGANG NA HIPON
(Shrimps in Tamarind Broth)

Makes 8 servings.

			Metric		English	
5	cups	**Water**	11/4 L		2 1/2	pints
1	pc	**Onion, medium-sized, quartered**	60	g	2	oz
2	pcs	**Tomatoes, sliced into wedges**	85	g	3	oz
1	pc	**_Labanos_ (radish), peeled and cut diagonally**	200	g	7	oz
1	cup	**_Sitaw_ (long beans), cut into 2" (4 cm) strips**	100	g	3 1/2	oz
2	pcs	**_Sili_ (green chili pepper)**	20	g	3/4	oz
1/2	tbsp	**_Patis_ (fish sauce)**	7	mL	1/4	fl oz
1	pouch	**Mama Sita's _Sinigang_ (Tamarind Seasoning) Mix**	25	g	1	oz
20-25	pcs	**_Sugpo_ (prawns), trimmed**	1/2 Kg		1.1	lbs
1	cup	**Green leafy vegetables such as _kangkong_ (asian watercress), spinach, or _mustasa_ (mustard greens)**	50	g	1 3/4	oz

1. Bring water to a boil. Add onion and tomatoes. Simmer for 5 minutes.

2. Add radish, long beans, chili pepper, fish sauce, and Mama Sita's Sinigang (Tamarind Seasoning) Mix. Continue to simmer for 3 minutes uncovered.

3. Add the shrimps and simmer for another 3 minutes. Turn off the heat and add the green leafy vegetables. Cover to steam-cook vegetables.

4. Serve immediately.

Variation: Fish or pre-boiled beef brisket may also be used instead of shrimps.

CALAMARES
(Squid Rings)

Makes 4 servings.

			Metric		English	
8	pcs	*Pusit* (squid)	1/2 Kg		1.1	lbs
1	pc	*Calamansi* or half slice of lemon	10	g	1/3	oz
1/2	cup	Mama Sita's *Palabok* (Shrimp Gravy) Mix	80	g	2 3/4	oz
1	cup	Cornstarch	120	g	4 1/4	oz
1	cup	Cooking oil	250	mL	8 1/2	fl oz

Dipping Sauce:

			Metric		English	
1	pouch	Mama Sita's Sweet & Sour Sauce Mix	57	g	2	oz
3/4	cup	Water	187	mL	6 1/3	fl oz

1. Clean the squid, remove the head, and cut into rings about 1/8" thick.

2. Squeeze calamansi or lemon over the squid, then wash thoroughly. Drain.

3. Combine Mama Sita's Palabok (Shrimp Gravy) Mix and cornstarch.

4. Roll squid rings lightly in the palabok-cornstarch mixture.

5. Deep fry until golden brown.

6. Serve with Mama Sita's Sweet and Sour Sauce or Mama Sita's Coconut Nectar Vinegar with crushed garlic, salt, and pepper.

Dipping Sauce:
1. Dissolve Mama Sita's Sweet and Sour Sauce Mix in 3/4 cup water.
2. Boil and simmer, stirring constantly for 2 minutes.

Variation: For a more fruity flavor, substitute 3/4 cup water with any of the following:
      a. juice from lemon diluted with 3/4 cup. water
      b. 1/2 cup Pineapple juice and 1/4 cup water

PAKSIW NA BANGUS
(Milkfish Poached In Vinegar & Spices)

<u>*Makes 4 servings.*</u>

			Metric		English	
1	pc	**Whole *Bangus* (Milkfish), sliced diagonally or *Banak* (mullet) may also be used**	1/2 Kg		1.1	lbs
1/4	cup+	**Mama Sita's Young Coconut**	68	mL	2 1/4	fl oz
1	tsp	**Vinegar** dissolved in:				
3/4	cup	**Water**	188	mL	6 1/3	fl oz
6	slices	**Ginger, pounded** approximately 3/4 " wide	20	g	3/4	oz
1	bulb	**Garlic, crushed**	30	g	1	oz
1	tsp	**Peppercorn**				
2	tsp	**Rock salt**	8	g	1/4	oz
1	tbsp	**Cooking oil (optional)**	15	mL	1/2	fl oz

1. *In a saucepan, combine together all ingredients except bangus. Bring to a boil.*
2. *Add the fish, lower the heat, and simmer until fish is cooked through.*
3. *Serve.*

TOCINONG ISDA
(Sweet Fish)

<u>*Makes 4 servings.*</u>

			Metric		English	
2	pcs	**Fish: *Bangus* (milkfish) or trout**	1/2 Kg		1.1	lbs
1	pouch	**Mama Sita's *Tocino* (Marinating) Mix**	75	g	2 2/3	oz
6	tbsp	**Cooking oil**	90	mL	3	fl oz

1. *Slit fish on the backside from head to tail, wash, and pat dry.*
2. *Sprinkle Mama Sita's Tocino (Marinating) Mix on the fish and rub it evenly over the flesh.*
3. *Marinate for at least 30 minutes.*
4. *Pan fry over medium heat.*

SOTANGHON SOUP
(Vermicelli Soup)

Makes 6 servings.

			Metric		English	
7	cups	Water	1 3/4 L		3 1/2	pints
15	pcs	Chicken neck	1	Kg	2.2	lbs
1	pc	Chicken liver	40	g	1 1/2	oz
1	pc	Chicken gizzard	45	Kg	1 1/2	oz
1/3	cup	Spring Onion, chopped	20	g	3/4	oz
1	tsp	Salt	5	g	1/4	oz
1/4	tsp	Black Pepper	1	g	1/28	oz
2	tbsp	Cooking oil	30	mL	1	fl oz
5	tbsp	Garlic, crushed	40	g	1 1/2	oz
1	pc	Onion, chopped	40	g	1 1/2	oz
2	tbsp	Mama Sita's *Caldereta* (Spicy Sauce) Mix	20	g	3/4	oz
2	tsp	Mama Sita's *Achuete* (Annatto) Powder	5	g	1/4	oz
1	pack	Sotanghon noodle (vermicelli)	100	g	3 1/2	oz
1 1/2	tsp	*Patis* (fish sauce)	8	mL	1/4	fl oz
1 1/2	tbsp	*Tenga ng Daga* (dried wood ear mushroom), soaked in 1/4 c. water and chopped	10	g	1/3	oz

Garnishing:

1/3	cup	*Dahon ng sibuyas* (spring onions), cut into strings	20	g	3/4	oz
5	tbsp	Garlic, fried until golden Calamansi	40	g	1 1/2	oz

1. In a 4 qt. saucepan. Combine chicken, water, spring onion, pepper, and salt. After 2 minutes, set aside the liver, lower the heat, and simmer until chicken meat is falling off the bone. (approximately 2 hrs.), leaving about 6 ¾ cups stock.
2. Remove the meat from the pan and flake.
3. Slice the liver and gizzard.
4. In a saucepan, sauté garlic in oil. As it turns golden, add onion.
5. As onion start to wilt, add the liver and gizzard. Stir fry.
6. Add Mama Sita's Achuette (Annatto) Powder and Mama Sita's Caldereta (SpicySauce) Mix. Stir-fry.
7. Pour in the soup stock and bring to a boil.
8. Add in the sotanghon and cook until done. Add dried mushroom and fish sauce to taste and mix in the shredded chicken meat. Serve with fried garlic, chopped spring onion, and calamansi.

Chicken

*"The Reyes name is one associated with fine
culinary tradition in thePhilippines."*

Nancy T Lu
The China Post, Taiwan
July 6, 1995

"Mama Sita...coming soon to a kitchen near you"

*"Clarita Reyes Lapus practically grew
up in the kitchen .
When her father lost his eyesight at the age of 36,
her mother, Teresita (Known in the Philippines
as the legendary "Mama Sita") had to sell
halo-halo (a popular summer refreshment in
the Philippines made from preserved fruits, leche flan
and ice shavings) and turon (deep-fried sugared
plantains wrapped in rice paper) to augment
the family income".*

Marie Feliciano
China News, Taiwan
July 6, 1995

"Joy to the lone expatriate comes in small food packets"

*"What the Lapuses did was to capture the essence
and flavors of favorite Filipino dishes in manufacturing
more than 10 kinds of sauces and mixes such as
meat stew mix for menudo and afritada
peanut sauce mix for kare-kare".*

Marie Feliciano, KABAYAN!
China News, Taiwan
July 9, 1995

SINAMPALUKANG MANOK
(Tamarind-Flavored Chicken Soup)

**Makes 4 servings.**

			Metric		English	
2	tbsp	**Cooking oil**	30	mL	1	fl oz
1	tbsp	**Garlic, crushed**	10	g	1/3	oz
1	pc	**Onion, sliced**	60	g	2	oz
1	pc	**Ginger, small, sliced**	10	g	1/3	oz
1	pc	**Tomato, sliced**	45	g	1 1/2	oz
3	cups	**Chicken, cut into serving pieces**	1/2 Kg		1.1	lbs
1	tbsp	_**Patis**_ **(fish sauce)**	15	mL	1/2	fl oz
3	cups	**Water**	750	mL	1 1/2	pints
2	tbsp	**Mama Sita's** _**Sinigang**_ **(Tamarind Seasoning) Mix**	30	g	1	oz
1	cup	_**Sitaw**_ **(long beans)**	100	g	3 1/2	oz
1	pc	_**Sili**_ **(long green pepper)**	10	g	1/3	oz

1. _Fry garlic in cooking oil. Add the onion, ginger, and tomato._

2. _Add the chicken, stir-fry, and season with fish sauce._

3. _When the chicken is almost done, add water and bring to a boil._

4. _Add Mama Sita's Sinigang (Tamarind Seasoning) Mix, long beans, and long green pepper. Continue cooking until the vegetables are ready._

5. _Serve with fish sauce._

CHICKEN AFRITADA
(Chicken Stewed with Potatoes and Bell Peppers)

Makes 3-4 servings.

			Metric		English	
2	tbsp	Cooking oil	30	mL	1	fl oz
3	cups	Chicken, cut into serving pieces	1/2	Kg	1.1	lbs
1	pouch	Mama Sita's *Menudo/Afritada* (Meat Stew) Mix, dissolved in:	30	g	1	oz
1	cup	Water	250	mL	8 1/2	fl oz
1	cup	Potatoes, cubed, fried	200	g	7	oz
2	pcs	Red and green bell pepper, cut into strips	100	g	3 1/2	oz
1/2	cup	Green peas (optional)	75	g	2 2/3	oz

1. *Stir-fry chicken until golden brown.*

2. *Pour dissolved Mama Sita's Menudo/Afritada (Meat Stew) Mix, simmer until tender. Add hot water if necessary.*

3. *Add fried potatoes, bell pepper, and green peas.*

4. *Simmer for 2 minutes.*

DICED CHICKEN WITH CASHEW NUTS

__Makes 4 servings__

Chicken Mixture:

			Metric		English	
2/3	cup	**Deboned chicken, diced**	100	g	3 1/2	oz
		Ground pepper to season				
1	tbsp	**Soy sauce**	15	mL	1/2	fl oz
1	tbsp	**Rhum**	15	mL	1/2	fl oz
1	tsp	**Cornstarch**	2	g	1/14	oz
2	tbsp	**Peanut oil or ordinary oil**	30	mL	1	fl oz
1	tbsp	**Garlic, minced**	10	g	1/3	oz
1	tbsp	**Ginger, minced**	20	g	3/4	oz

Seasoned Broth:

			Metric		English	
1	cup	**Chicken broth**	250	mL	8 1/2	fl oz
1	tsp	**Sugar**	4	g	1/8	oz
1 1/2	tbsp	**Mama Sita's Oyster Sauce**	30	g	1	oz
2	tsp	**Cornstarch**	4	g	1/8	oz
1/2	cup	***Chicharo***	50	g	1 3/4	oz
1/2	cup	**Sweet peas**	90	g	3 1/8	oz
1/2	cup	**Toasted cashew halves**	100	g	3 1/2	oz
		Drops of sesame oil				
		Salt and pepper to taste				

1. *Combine ingredients for the chicken mixture. Let stand for several minutes.*

2. *Sauté the garlic and ginger in oil. Add the chicken mixture and stir-fry until chicken is half-cooked.*

3. *Combine broth, sugar, Mama Sita's Oyster Sauce, cornstarch and pour into chicken mixture. Continue cooking until chicken is tender.*

4. *Add the vegetables, cashew, and drops of sesame oil. Season to taste with salt and pepper.*

5. *Serve hot.*

CHICKEN TWIST

Makes 4-6 servings.

			Metric		English	
3	cups	**Boneless chicken breast, skinned**	1/2 Kg		1.1	lbs
2	tbsp	**Mama Sita's _Caldereta_ (Spicy Sauce) Mix**	20	g	3/4	oz
1	cup	**All-purpose flour**	150	g	5 1/4	oz
2	pcs	**Eggs, beaten**	120	g	4 1/4	oz
1	cup	**Bread crumbs**	150	g	5 1/4	oz
1/2	cup	**Cooking oil**	125	mL	4 1/4	fl oz

Dipping Sauce:

1	pouch	**Mama Sita's Sweet & Sour Sauce Mix**	57	g	2	oz
3/4	cup	**Water**	187	mL	6 1/3	fl oz

1. _With the flat side of a meat mallet or rolling pin, pound chicken lightly until 1/4" thick. Cut diagonally into strips, about 4"x 1"._
2. _Sprinkle Mama Sita's Caldereta (Spicy Sauce) Mix and rub it evenly over the meat. Marinate for about 30 minutes._
3. _Dip each piece in flour, shaking off excess._
4. _Dip chicken in beaten egg, and roll in breadcrumbs._
5. _Gently twist each strip several times. Chill chicken pieces for 30 minutes._
6. _Heat cooking oil to 365°F and fry chicken five pieces at a time until golden brown._
7. _Drain well on paper towels._
8. _Serve with Mama Sita's Sweet & Sour Sauce._

To Make Sauce:
Dissolve Mama Sita's Sweet & Sour Sauce Mix in water. Boil and simmer, stirring constantly for 2 minutes.

CHICKEN POT PIE

			Metric		*English*	
2	tsp	Garlic, crushed	10	g	1/3	oz
1 1/2	tbsp	Onion, sliced	25	g	3/4	oz
2	cups	Chicken meat, cut into cubes (approximately 1"x1" inch)	1/2	g	1.1	lbs
1	pouch	Mama Sita's *Menudo Afritada* (Meat Stew) Mix, dissolved in:	30	g	1	oz
1	cup	Water	250	mL	8 1/2	fl oz
2	stalks	Celery, cut finely	10	g	2	stalks
1	cup	Carrots, diced (1/2"x1/2")	2	g	1/14	oz
3/4	cup	Potatoes, diced (1/2"x1/2") Salt to taste	155	g	1 1/2	fl oz

1. In a pan sauté garlic and onion in cooking oil.
2. As the onions start to wilt, add chicken meat and stir-fry.
3. Add Mama Sita's Menudo Afritada (Meat Stew) Mix and celery. Cook covered for 5 minutes.
4. Add potatoes and carrots. Cover again and cook until done, adding water to prevent it from drying up. Add salt to taste. Transfer onto a greased ovenproof dish.

Pie Crust: Follow the same procedure as for the crust of Tuna Empanada on p.35.

To Assemble:
Roll the dough into the shape of ovenproof dish and place it on top of the chicken, touching the edges against the sides of the pan. Prick edges with a fork, brush with beaten eggyolk and bake at 350°F for 15 minutes or until golden.

CHICKEN LOLLIPOP

<u>*Makes 34 servings.*</u>

			Metric		*English*	
17	pcs	**Chicken wings**	1	Kg	2.2	lbs
1	pouch	**Mama Sita's *Caldereta* (Spicy Sauce) Mix**	50	g	1 3/4	oz
2	pcs	**Eggs**	120	g	4 1/4	oz
1 2/3	cups	**All-purpose flour**	1/4	Kg	9	oz
1	cup	**Breadcrumbs**	150	g	5 1/4	oz
4	cups	**Cooking oil**	1	L	1	quart
		Salt to taste				

1. *Cut each wing on the joint and scrape off the meat to one end to form a "lollipop."*

2. *Marinate in Mama Sita's Caldereta (Spicy Sauce) Mix for 30 minutes.*

3. *Dip in beaten eggs, dredge in flour and roll in breadcrumbs.*

4. *Deep fry over medium heat and drain on paper towels.*

Variation: Marinate chicken in 1/2 cup Mama Sita's Barbecue Marinade overnight.

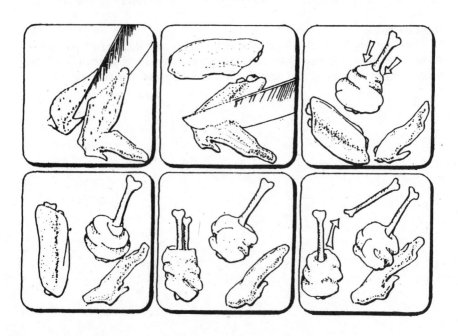

PASTEL DE POLLO
(Chicken Stew with Pastry Crust)

Makes 6-8 servings.

Chicken mixture:

			Metric		English	
6	tbsp	Cooking oil	90	mL	3	fl oz
1 1/4	cups	Potatoes, cubed	1/4	Kg	9	oz
1 1/4	cups	Carrots, cubed	1/4	Kg	9	oz
1	cup	*Sibuyas Tagalog* (shallots), chopped finely	150	g	5 1/4	oz
6	cups	Chicken meat, diced	1	Kg	2.2	lbs
1	pouch	Mama Sita's *Caldereta* (Spicy Sauce) Mix, dissolved in:	50	g	1 3/4	oz
1/4	cup	Water	62	mL	2	fl oz
1 1/2	cups	Mushroom, quartered (optional)	150	g	5 1/4	oz
1/2	cup	Grated cheese	80	g	2 3/4	oz
1	cup	Cream (optional)	1/4	Kg	9	oz

1. *Fry potatoes and carrots.*

2. *In another pan, sauté shallots in cooking oil.*

3. *Add the chicken and stir until the edges turn brown.*

4. *Add Mama Sita's Caldereta (Spicy Sauce) Mix dissolved in water and cook until the chicken is tender.*

5. *Add potatoes, carrots, mushrooms, and cheese.*

6. *Stir over low fire until the cheese has melted.*

7. *Turn off the heat and stir in the cream.*

Pie Crust:

2 1/4	cups	Sifted all-purpose flour	337	g	12	oz
1/4	tsp	Salt	1	g	1/28	oz
10	tbsp	Shortening	150	g	5 1/4	oz
1/3	cup	Ice-cold water	83	mL	2 3/4	fl oz
1	pc	Eggyolk, beaten	35	g	1 1/4	oz

1. *Sift flour and salt into a bowl.*

2. *With two knives or a pastry blender, cut half of the shortening into the flour mixture until the shortening has been well covered with flour. Then cut in the remaining shortening until the dough is sandy.*

3. *Sprinkle about 4 tbsp of water into the dough and gently blend it in. Little by little, add as much of the remaining water as necessary.*

4. *Gather the dough into a ball and roll out to the shape of the oven proof baking dish.*

To Assemble:

1. *Pour chicken mixture into an ovenproof dish.*

2. *Top with crust and pinch the edges to seal.*

3. *Prick the crust with a fork, brush with the beaten eggyolk, and bake at 350°F until golden brown (about 15 minutes).*

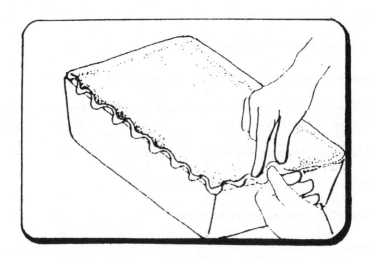

MAMA SITA'S VERSION OF ADOBONG ILONGGO

			Metric		English	
3	cups	**Chicken, cut into** serving pieces	1/2	Kg	1.1	lbs
3	cups	**Pork** _liempo_**, cut into** serving pieces	1/2	Kg	1.1	lbs
1	tsp	**Garlic, crushed**	10	g	1/3	oz
2	slices	**Ginger, crushed**	5	g	1/4	oz
1	pc	**Onion, sliced**	30	g	1	oz
1	tsp	**Whole peppercorn**	1	g	1/28	oz
3/4	tbsp	**Rock salt**	11	g	1/3	oz
1/3	cup	**Mama Sita's Coconut Nectar** **Vinegar**	83	mL	2 3/4	fl oz
1/2	cup	**Water**	125	mL	4 1/4	fl oz
1	tsp	**Mama Sita's** _Achuete_ **(Annatto) Powder**	3	g	3/28	oz

1. _In a small bowl, combine all ingredients except chicken, pork, and Mama Sita's Achuete (Annatto)._

2. _In a wok approximately 12" in diameter and 4" deep, place the pork and chicken, taking care that all the pork is closer to the bottom of the pan._

3. _Pour in the rest of the ingredients. Bring to a boil and lower the heat to simmer until tender._

4. _Dissolve Mama Sita's Achuete (Annatto) Powder in 1 tbsp of water and mix into the meat._

5. _Continue cooking until the oil comes out, and mix very well._

ADOBONG MANOK
(Chicken in Savory Sauce)

Makes 4 servings.

			Metric		English	
3	cups	**Chicken or pork, cut into serving pieces**	1/2	kg	1	lb
1	pouch	**Mama Sita's Savory Sauce (*Adobo*)**	25	g	3/4	oz
		Mix dissolved in:				
	1/4 cup	**Water**	60	mL	2	fl oz

1. *In a casserole, combine the meat and the dissolved Mama Sita's Adobo (Savory Sauce) Mix. Cook over medium heat. When the sauce starts to boil, lower the heat and simmer. Stir once in a while to prevent the sauce from sticking to the pan.*

2. *Continue cooking until the meat is tender and the sauce is slightly thick.*

3. *Remove from heat and serve with steamed rice.*

CHICKEN POT, ADOBO STYLE
by Iris Lonergan

Second Prize Winner, Pistang-Pista Sa Mama Sita Cooking Contest
Amsterdam, The Netherlands

<u>*Makes 6-8 servings.*</u>

			Metric		English	
2	tbsp	Cooking oil or margarine	30	mL	1	fl oz
2	tsp	Garlic, crushed	6	g	1/4	oz
2	pcs	Onion, medium-sized, sliced thinly	120	g	4 1/4	oz
9	cups	Chicken, cut into small pieces	1 1/2 Kg		3.3	lbs
1	pouch	Mama Sita's *Adobo* (Savory Sauce) Mix	50	g	1 3/4	oz
1	pc	Ginger, small, crushed	10	g	1/3	oz
2	stalks	Lemon grass	30	g	1	oz
1	can	Whole tomatoes	400	g	14 1/2	oz
1	cup	Water	250	mL	8 1/2	fl oz
1	tsp	Salt	4	g	1/8	oz

1. Sauté the garlic and onions in oil or margarine. Add chicken.

2. Add Mama Sita's Adobo (Savory Sauce) Mix and the rest of the ingredients.
    Bring to a boil and simmer until chicken cutlets are tender.

Optional: *Add 1 green pepper or 150g of snow peas or 2 steamed carrots.*

SARSIADONG ITLOG

(Boiled Eggs With Spicy Tomato Sauce)
by Mellie van Vulpen-Lacson

First Prize Winner, Pistang-Pista Sa Mama Sita Cooking Contest
Amsterdam, The Netherlands

<u>**Makes 4 servings.**</u>

			Metric		English	
1	tsp	**Garlic, crushed**	3	g	3/28	oz
1	pc	**Onion, chopped**	60	g	2	oz
3	pcs	**Tomatoes, chopped**	150	g	9 1/2	oz
2	tbsp	**Cooking oil**	30	mL	1	fl oz
1	pouch	**Mama Sita's** *Caldereta* **(Spicy Sauce) Mix, dissolved in:**	50	g	1 3/4	oz
1	cup	**Water**	250	mL	8 1/2	fl oz
1/4	tsp	**Salt**	1	g	1/28	oz
1/4	cup	**Kim's Sweet Chili Sauce**	62	mL	2 1/2	fl oz
1	pc	**Eggplant, big, cut into rounds and fried**	67	g	2 1/3	oz
4	pcs	**Eggs, hard boiled, peeled and halved crosswise**	240	g	8	oz

1. *Sauté garlic, onion, and tomatoes in cooking oil.*

2. *Add salt and the dissolved Mama Sita's Caldereta (Spicy Sauce) Mix. Boil for 3 minutes while stirring constantly.*

3. *Pour the sauce in a platter. Arrange fried eggplant over the sauce and top with Kim's Sweet Chili Sauce and halved boiled eggs.*

Tip: To boil eggs without breaking, add a little salt or a drop of vinegar in the water or puncture top of eggs before boiling.

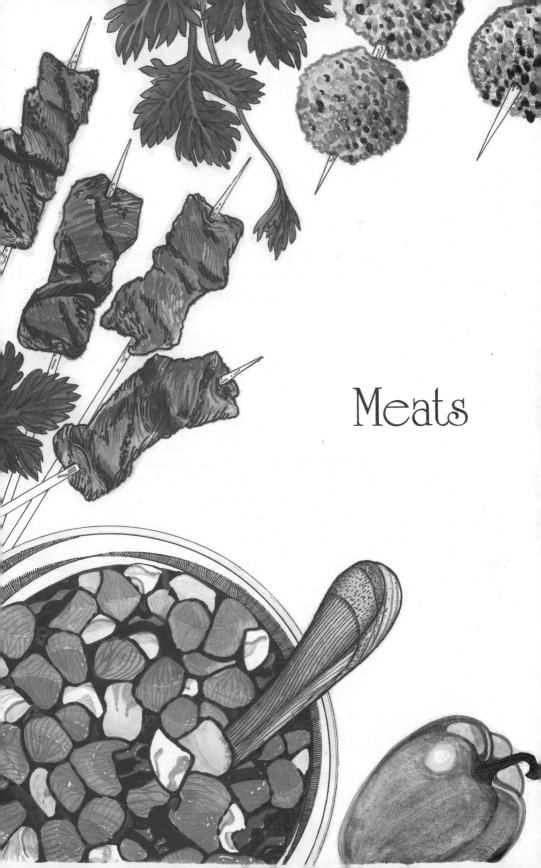

Meats

*"Filipinos living overseas can now savour
'genuine home food' through
Mama Sita's sauces and mixes."*

*"The Kare-kare definitely evokes a great
deal of response - either you love it or
dislike it passionately."*

PINSEC FRITO
(Crispy Wontons)

Makes 6-8 servings

Filling:

			Metric		English	
1 1/2	cups	**Ground pork**	1/4	Kg	9	oz
2 1/2	tbsp	***Dahon ng sibuyas* (spring onion), chopped finely**	5	g	1/4	oz
1	pc	**Egg, beaten**	60	g	2	oz
3	tbsp	**All-purpose flour**	28	g	1	oz
1	tbsp	**Cornstarch**	7	g	1/4	oz
2	tsp	**Mama Sita's *Adobo* (Savory Sauce) Mix**	5	g	1/8	oz
1	tbsp	**Mama Sita's Oyster Sauce**	20	g	3/4	oz
50	pcs	**Wonton wrapper**	(9cmx9cm)(3 1/2"x3 1/2")			
2	cups	**Cooking oil, for deep frying**	500	mL	1	pint
1	pouch	**Mama Sita's Sweet & Sour Sauce Mix**	57	g	2	oz

1. *Combine the ingredients for the filling and mix thoroughly.*

2. *Scoop one teaspoon of the mixture onto each wonton wrapper. Moisten edges. Seal together by pressing, any two opposite corners to make a triangle. Join the moistened edges of the two corners at the base of the triangle to the third corner.*

3. *Deep fry over low flame until light brown. Place on a paper towel or strainer to drain excess oil.*

4. *Serve with Mama Sita's Sweet & Sour Sauce.*

Sweet & Sour Sauce Preparation: (See page 40.)

NAIIBANG LUMPIA
(Vietnamese Spring Rolls)

Makes 6-8 servings.

Filling:

			Metric		English	
1	pack	*Sotanghon* noodle (vermicelli), soaked, blanched, and cut into 3" (17cm) lengths	100	g	3 1/2	oz
2	tsp	*Tenga ng Daga* (dried tree ear mushroom), soaked and coarsely chopped	2	g	1/14	oz
1/2	cup	*Singkamas* (jicama), chopped	50	g	1 3/4	oz
2	tsp	Garlic, crushed	6	g	1/4	oz
1	pc	Onion, chopped	60	g	2	oz
1	tbsp	Mama Sita's Oyster Sauce	20	g	3/4	oz
1	pouch	Mama Sita's Barbecue Marinade Mix	50	g	1 3/4	oz
3	pcs	Eggs	180	g	6 1/3	oz
3	cups	Ground pork	1/2	Kg	1.1	lbs
15	pcs	*Lumpia* (spring roll) wrappers (12 cm dia)			(4 3/4" dia)	
		Oil for deep frying				

1. Combine filling ingredients in a bowl and mix thoroughly.

2. Scoop two tablespoonfuls onto each lumpia wrapper, roll, and seal.

3. Deep fry and drain.

4. Serve with dipping sauce.

Dipping Sauce:

2	tbsp	Grated carrots	20	g	3/4	oz
1	tbsp	Grated radish	10	g	1/3	oz
2	tbsp	Calamansi juice	30	mL	1	fl oz
2	tbsp	Sugar	26	g	1	oz
1/4	cup	*Patis* (fish sauce)	62	mL	2	fl oz
1/4	cup	Mama Sita's *Sukang Tuba* (All Natural Vinegar)	62	mL	2	fl oz
1	tbsp	Garlic, crushed	9	g	3/8	oz

Combine all ingredients and stir.

BARBECUE

The classic favorite made easy!

Makes about 20 barbecue sticks.

			Metric		English	
6	cups	**Kasim (pork shoulder), cut** into 2"x1"x 1/4" strips. (Sirloin steak, lamb, shrimp, scallops, calamari or fish fillet may also be used.)	1	Kg	2.2	lbs
1/2	cup	**Mama Sita's Barbecue** **Marinade** **Cooking oil for basting**	125	mL	4 1/4	fl oz

1. *In a bowl, combine pieces of meat and Mama Sita's Barbecue Marinade.*

2. *Marinate for at least 3 hours. If using shrimp, scallops, calamari or fish fillet, marinate for just 10 minutes. When ready to grill, skew meat with bamboo sticks.*

3. *Grill over live charcoal about 2-3 minutes on each side or to desired doneness.*

4. *Brush occasionally with the marinade mixed with cooking oil.*

LONGANISA
(Breakfast Sausage)

Makes 6 pieces.

			Metric		English	
1 1/2	cups	**Ground pork**	1/4 Kg		9	oz
1	pouch	**Mama Sita's *Tocino* (Marinating) Mix**	75	g	2 2/3	oz
2	tsp	**Garlic, crushed and chopped**	6	g	1/4	oz
1/4	tsp	**Black pepper**	1	g	1/28	oz
1/4	tsp	**Salt**	1	g	1/28	oz

1. *Combine all ingredients in a bowl. Mix thoroughly. Let stand in the refrigerator for at least one hour.*

2. *Roll the mixture two tablespoons at a time in wax paper. Refrigerate for another hour.*

3. *Remove from wax paper and fry in hot oil until brown.*

4. *Serve hot.*

Note: This can be stored in the freezer. Thaw before frying.

PAKSIW NA LECHON
(Pork Stewed in Tangy Liver Sauce)

Makes 4-6 servings.

			Metric		English	
1/4	Kg	*Lechon* (roast pork), cut into serving pieces	250	g	1/2	lb
1	cup	Water	250	mL	8 1/2	fl oz
1	pc	*Laurel* leaves				
1	bottle	Mama Sita's *Sarsa ng Lechon* (Sauce for Roasts) Regular	312	g	11	oz
1	tbsp	Mama Sita's Coco Floral Sap (All Natural Vinegar)	15	mL	1/2	fl oz
1/2	tsp	Peppercorn, whole	2	g	1/14	oz
1 1/2	tbsp	Sugar	15	g	1/2	oz

1. In a small saucepan, combine all ingredients and cook over medium flame.

2. Bring to a boil and lower the heat.

3. Gently simmer for 15 minutes or until the desired thickness is achieved. Season with salt if necessary.

MECHADO
(Beef Braised in Savory Shallot Sauce)

<u>*Makes 6-8 servings.*</u>

			Metric		English	
1	Kg	**Kabilugan or Punta y pecho** (whole beef round or beef brisket or spare ribs)	1	Kg	2.2	lbs
1	strip	**Pork fat, cut into strips** (optional, use only if you will be using *kabilugan*)	165	g	5 3/4	oz
1	pouch	**Mama Sita's** *Adobo* **(Savory Sauce) Mix, dissolved in:**	50	g	1 3/4	oz
1	cup	**Water**	250	mL	8 1/2	fl oz
1/2	cup	**Cooking oil**	125	mL	4 1/4	fl oz
6 1/2	cups	*Sibuyas Tagalog* **(shallots)** or any other kind of onion, chopped finely	1	Kg	2.2	lbs
1/2	tsp	**Mama Sita's** *Achuete* **(Annatto) Powder** **Salt to taste**	1	g	1/28	oz
1	cup	**Potatoes, cubed and fried**	200	g	7	oz

1. *Lard the beef by cutting through with a thin knife and inserting fat strips. (Beef spare ribs may also be used.)*

2. *Marinate beef in dissolved Mama Sita's Adobo (Savory Sauce) Mix for at least 4 hours.*

3. *Sauté the shallots and set aside.*

4. *In the same oil, fry the beef until it is well browned. Add shallots, Mama Sita's Achuete (Annatto) Powder, marinade, and salt. Cover and simmer. Add water if necessary. Reduce heat. Stir once in a while.*

5. *Add potatoes when meat is tender. Slice meat crosswise. Arrange on a platter. Pour sauce over meat and potatoes.*

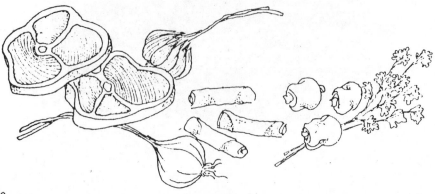

ADOBO IN COCOSAUCE

Makes 4 servings.

			Metric		English	
3	cups	**Pork or chicken, cut into serving pieces**	1/2 Kg		1.1	lbs
1	pouch	**Mama Sita's** *Adobo* **(Savory Sauce) Mix, dissolved in:**	25	g	3/4	oz
1/4	cup	**Water**	62	mL	2	fl oz
1/4	cup	***Gata* (Coconut milk)**	62	mL	2	fl oz

1. *In a casserole, combine the meat and the dissolved Mama Sita's Adobo (Savory Sauce) Mix. Cook over medium heat. When the sauce starts to boil, lower the heat and simmer.*

2. *When the meat is half-cooked, add the coconut milk. Stir once in a while to prevent the sauce from sticking to the pan.*

3. *Continue cooking until the meat is tender and the sauce is slightly thick.*

4. *Remove from heat and serve with steamed rice.*

PAKSIW NA PATA
(Pickled Pork Hocks)

Makes 5 servings.

			Metric		English	
6	cups	*Pata* (pork hocks), medium-sized, cut into pieces	1	Kg	2.2	lbs
1/4	cup	**Mama Sita's Coconut Nectar Vinegar**	62	mL	2	fl oz
1	tbsp	**Garlic, crushed**	10	g	1/3	fl oz
1/2	cup	**Dried *bulaklak ng saging* (banana blossoms), soaked in:**	40	g	1 1/2	oz
1	cup	**Water**	250	mL	8 1/2	fl oz
8	pcs	**Peppercorn, whole**	1	g	1/28	oz
2	pcs	**Bay leaves**	1	g	1/28	oz
1/3	cup	**Mama Sita's Barbecue Marinade**	83	mL	2 3/4	fl oz
2	cups	**Water**	500	mL	1	pint

1. Combine all ingredients.

2. Boil then simmer for one hour or longer until tender. Stir once in a while to prevent from sticking to the casserole.

PORK ASADO
(Sweet Pork Stew)

Makes 8 servings.

			Metric		English	
1	Kg	**Pork Shoulder**	1	Kg	2.2	lbs
1	cup	**Water**	250	mL	8 1/2	fl oz
1/2	cup	**Mama Sita's Barbecue Marinade**	125	mL	4 1/4	fl oz
2	tbsp	**Rhum**	30	mL	1	fl oz
2	tbsp	**Sugar**	26	g	1	oz
2	pcs	**Bay leaves**	1	g	1/28	oz
1	tbsp	**Cornstarch, dissolved in:**	7	g	1/4	oz
3	tbsp	**Water**	45	mL	1 1/2	fl oz

1. *Combine pork, water, Mama Sita's Barbecue Marinade, rhum, sugar, and bay leaves. Bring to a boil.*

2. *Lower the heat and simmer until the pork is tender.*

3. *Remove the meat and slice thinly.*

4. *Thicken the sauce with the cornstarch and water mixture.*

5. *Pour the sauce over the meat.*

6. *Serve.*

PATA HUMBA
(Pork Hocks Stew)

			Metric		English	
1/4	cup	Cooking oil	62	mL	2	fl oz
4	pcs	*Saba* banana, sliced	200	g	7	oz
1	pc	*Pata* (hind quarter),	1	Kg	2.2	lbs
1/2	cup	Mama Sita's Barbecue Marinade	125	mL	4 1/4	fl oz
3	tbsp	*Calamansi* (lemon) juice	45	mL	1 1/2	fl oz
6	cups	Water	1 1/2 L		3	pints
2	pcs	Oregano leaves	1	g	1/28	oz
2	pcs	Laurel leaves	1	g	1/28	oz
2	tsp	Garlic, crushed	6	g	1/4	oz
1	petal	Star anise	2	g	1/14	oz
1	tsp	Brown sugar	5	g	1/8	oz
1	tbsp	Cornstarch, dissolved in:	7	g	1/4	oz
1/4	cup	Water	62	mL	2	fl oz
1	tsp	Mama Sita's Oyster Sauce	7	g	1/4	oz
3	pcs	Eggs, boiled and halved	180	g	6 1/3	oz

1. *Fry banana in cooking oil. Set aside.*

2. *In a saucepan, marinate pata in Mama Sita's Barbecue Marinade and calamansi juice for 2 hours, turning occasionally.*

3. *Add water, oregano leaves, bay leaves, garlic, and star anise.*

4. *Boil and simmer until tender.*

5. *Add brown sugar, dissolved cornstarch and Mama Sita's Oyster Sauce. Stir and simmer until sauce thickens.*

6. *When almost done, add boiled eggs.*

7. *Garnish with fried banana.*

KARE-KARE
(Oxtail in Rich Peanut Sauce)

Makes 4-5 servings.

			Metric		English	
3	cups	_Buntot ng baka_ (oxtail), cleaned and cut into serving pieces	1/2	Kg	1.1	lbs
1	tsp	**Garlic, crushed**	3	g	3/28	oz
1	pc	**Onion, sliced**	60	g	2	oz
1	cup	**Eggplant, cut diagonally into 1" lengths**	200	g	7	oz
1	cup	_Sitaw_ (long green beans), cut into 2" pieces	100	g	3 1/2	oz
1	bundle	_Pechay_ (bok choy)	100	g	3 1/2	oz
1	pouch	**Mama Sita's _Kare-Kare_ (Peanut Sauce) Mix**	57	g	2	oz
1	tbsp	**Cooking oil**	15	mL	1/2	fl oz
1/2	cup	_Bagoong alamang_ (Sauteed shrimp fry)	50	g	1 3/4	oz

1. _Boil oxtail in 8 cups (2Litres) water and simmer until meat is tender leaving about 1 1/2 cup (375mL) stock. Set aside._

2. _Sauté garlic and onion. Add oxtail, and Mama Sita's Kare-Kare (Peanut Sauce) Mix dissolved in 1 cup water. Add remaining stock. Stir and simmer for 2 minutes._

3. _Add eggplant and string beans. Simmer for 3 minutes. Stir once in a while to prevent sauce from sticking to the pan._

4. _Add bok choy and simmer for 2 minutes or until vegetables are done._

5. _Serve with Bagoong alamang (sautéed shrimp fry)._

Variation:
Pressure cook 1/2 Kg oxtail for 45 minutes to 1 hour with 3-4 cups water.

LECHON KAWALI
(Crispy Pork)

			Metric		English	
6	cups	**Pork *liempo* (side bacon with rind)**	1	Kg	2.2	lbs
4	cups	**Water**	1	L	1	quart
		Salt to taste				
4	cups	**Cooking oil**	1	L	1	quart
1	bottle	**Mama Sita's *Sarsa ng Lechon* (Sauce for Roasts)**	312	g	11	oz

1. *Combine pork, water, and salt in a saucepan. Bring to a boil.*

2. *Lower the heat and simmer until the pork is tender. Drain the pork and cool.*

3. *Prick skin with fork and rub with salt. Leave in colander to dry for one hour.*

4. *Heat cooking oil in a deep fryer or wok at high heat. Fry pork until golden brown and crispy. Cut into serving pieces and serve with Mama Sita's Sarsa ng Lechon (Sauce for Roasts).*

SWEET AND SOUR PORK

			Metric		English	
3	cups	Pork tenderloin, cut across the grain into 2"x1/2" strips	1/2	Kg	1.1	lbs
3	tbsp	Soy sauce	45	mL	1 1/2	fl oz

Batter:

1	cup	Flour	150	g	5 1/4	oz
1/2	cup	Cornstarch	60	g	2	oz
1	tsp	Salt	4	g	1/8	oz
3/4	cup	Water	187	mL	6 1/3	fl oz
2	cups	Cooking oil	500	mL	1	pint
2	pcs	Green bell peppers, medium-sized, cut into wedges	100	g	3 1/2	oz
2	pcs	Red bell peppers, medium-, sized, cut into wedges	100	g	3 1/2	oz
1/2	cup	Carrots, medium-sized, cut into strips	100	g	3 1/2	oz
1	pc	Onion, medium-sized, cut into wedges	60	g	2	oz
1/2	cup	Pineapple chunks, drained, reserve 1 1/2cups (2 oz) pineapple juice and dilute with:	50	g	1 3/4	oz
1/2	cup	Water	125	mL	4 1/4	fl oz
1	pouch	Mama Sita's Sweet & Sour Sauce Mix	57	g	2	oz

1. *Marinate pork in soy sauce.*
2. *Combine flour, cornstarch, salt, and water. Mix well to form a thin paste. Add pork and coat evenly with batter.*
3. *Heat oil over medium heat. Deep fry pork until golden brown. Place in a strainer to drain excess oil.*
4. *Place pork in a saucepan, combine vegetables, pineapple juice, pineapple chunks, and Mama Sita's Sweet & Sour Mix. Bring to a slow boil while stirring constantly until sauce thickens. Serve on a platter.*

WONTON SOUP

Makes 6 servings.

Soup stock:

			Metric		English	
1	pc	**Pork or Chicken bones**	1/2	Kg	1.1	lbs
2	tbsp	**Cooking Oil**	30	mL	1	fl oz
1	pc	**Onion, quartered**	60	g	2	oz
1 1/2	cups	**Carrots, diced**	150	g	5 1/4	oz
1/4	cup	**Celery**	45	g	1 1/2	oz
2	tbsp	**Leeks**	15	g	1/2	oz
8	cups	**Water**	2	L	2	quarts
1	tbsp	**Salt**	12	g	3/8	oz
1/4	tsp	**Black pepper**	1	g	1/28	oz

Wonton filling:

			Metric		English	
3/4	cup	**Shrimps, shelled, deveined and chopped**	125	g	4 1/3	oz
3/4	cup	**Ground pork**	125	g	4 1/3	oz
1	tbsp	_Dahon ng sibuyas_ (spring onions), chopped	2	g	1/14	oz
2	tbsp	**Mama Sita's Oyster Sauce**	40	g	1 1/2	oz
2	tsp	**Garlic, chopped**	6	g	1/4	oz
1/4	tsp	**Ginger, chopped**	2	g	1/14	oz
30	pcs	**Wonton wrapper**	(9cmx9cm)	(3 1/2"x3 1/2")		
1	pc	**Egg, beaten**	60	g	2	oz
1/4	tsp	**Black pepper**	1	g	1/28	oz
		Dahon ng sibuyas (spring onions), chopped for garnish				

Soup Stock Cooking Directions:

1. _Brown pork bones (either bake it in a 350 °F oven for 10-15 minutes or fry it in 1/4 cup or 2 fl oz cooking oil). Set aside. In a saucepan, heat oil and sauté onion. Add carrots, celery, leeks, and browned pork bones._
2. _Add water, salt, and pepper. Let boil then simmer for 2 to 3 hours. Strain and set aside soup stock._

Wonton Soup Cooking directions:

1. *In a bowl, combine ingredients for the filling and mix thoroughly.*

2. *Scoop one teaspoon of the mixture onto each wonton wrapper. Moisten edges. Seal together by pressing, any two opposite corners to make a triangle. Join the moistened edges of the two corners at the base of the triangle to the third corner.*

3. *Measure 7 cups (1.8L) of soup stock into a saucepan and let boil.*

4. *Drop the dumplings, 5-6 at a time and cook for 5 minutes. Set aside. (Do not overload in pan to avoid clinging together. Repeat until the dumplings are cooked.)*

5. *Bring soup stock to a boil and add the fresh egg. Stir.*

6. *Drop the cooked dumplings and bring to a boil once more. Sprinkle with spring onions and pepper.*

7. *Serve hot.*

MEATBALLS IN WHITE SAUCE

Makes 6 servings. (25-30 meatballs)

Meatballs:

			Metric		English	
2	slices	**Loaf bread, chopped finely**	35	g	1 1/4	oz
1/2	cup	**Milk**	125	mL	4 1/4	fl oz
1 1/2	cups	**Ground pork**	1/4	Kg	9	oz
1 1/2	cups	**Ground beef**	1/4	Kg	9	oz
2	pcs	**Eggs, slightly beaten**	120	g	4 1/4	oz
1	pc	**Onion, chopped**	60	g	2	oz
1	pouch	**Mama Sita's Barbecue Marinade Mix**	50	g	1 3/4	oz
1	tsp	**Salt**	4	g	1/8	oz
5	tbsp	***Dahon ng sibuyas* (spring onions), chopped**	10	g	1/8	oz
1	cup	**Cooking oil, for frying**	250	mL	8 1/2	fl oz

White Sauce:

			Metric		English	
2	tbsp	**Butter**	30	g	1	oz
2	tbsp	**All-purpose flour**	18	g	2/3	oz
3/4	cup	**Soup stock**	187	mL	6 1/3	fl oz
1/2	cup	**Milk**	125	mL	4 1/4	fl oz

1. *In a large bowl, soak chopped bread in milk. Stir with a fork and let stand at room temperature for 5 minutes so that the bread can absorb the milk.*

2. *Add the rest of the meatball ingredients and toss the mixture with a fork until thoroughly combined.*

3. *Shape into balls.*

4. *Fry meatballs in cooking oil 15 pieces at a time for 10 minutes, turning frequently until brown on all sides and cooked through. Place on a paper towel or strainer to drain off excess oil. Set aside.*

White Sauce:

1. *Heat the pan and melt the butter.*

2. *Add the flour to the butter all at once and stir with a wooden spoon until smooth.*

3. *Add the soup stock while stirring constantly.*

4. *Set the fire to medium heat and bring flour mixture to a boil, stirring until mixture is smooth.*

5. *Add meatballs to the white sauce; toss gently to coat well. Remove from heat and serve.*

BAKED SPARE RIBS

<u>*Makes 6 servings.*</u>

			Metric		English	
6	cups	**Spare Ribs (choose meaty ribs)**	1	Kg	2.2	lbs
1/2	cup	**Mama Sita's Barbecue Marinade**	125	mL	4 1/4	fl oz

1. *Boil ribs in just enough water to cover it until it becomes tender. Drain.*

2. *Marinate in Mama Sita's Barbecue Marinade for 30 minutes.*

3. *Preheat oven at 180°C (350°F).*

4. *Bake ribs for 20 minutes.*

BEEF SINIGANG
(Beef in Tamarind Broth)

Makes 4-6 servings.

			Metric		English	
6	cups	**Water**	1 1/2	L	1 1/2	quarts
3	cups	**Stewing beef, preferably beef brisket, bone-in or beef short ribs, cut into chunks (pork, fish, shrimp, or scallops may also be used)**	1/2	Kg	1.1	lbs
5	tbsp	**Mama Sita's _Biglang Sinigang_ (Tamarind Paste)**	100	g	3 1/2	oz
1	pc	**Onion, quartered**	60	g	2	oz
2	pcs	**Tomato, sliced into 1" wedges**	90	g	3	oz
2	pcs	**Radish, peeled and cut into 1/4" diagonal slices**	200	g	7	oz
1	cup	**Green leafy vegetables (like _kangkong_, spinach, or mustard greens)**	20	g	3/4	oz
1	cup	**_Sitaw_ (long beans), cut into 2" strips**	100	g	3 1/2	oz
2	pcs	**_Sili_ (green chili pepper)**	20	g	3/4	oz
1	tsp	**_Patis_ (fish sauce)**	5	mL	1/8	fl oz

1. *Boil beef until tender, leaving about 4 cups broth.*

2. *Add Mama Sita's Biglang Sinigang (Tamarind Paste) and stir until well blended.*

3. *Add onion, tomatoes, and radish. Let boil until vegetables are almost done.*

4. *Add leafy vegetables, long beans, and green chili pepper last.*

5. *Add patis.*

BEEF WITH ASPARAGUS

Makes 2-3 servings.

			Metric		English	
3/4	cup	**Beef sirloin, pounded with the back of a knife and cut into strips**	150	g	5 1/4	oz
3	tbsp	**Mama Sita's Oyster Sauce**	60	g	2 1/4	oz
1	tbsp	**Garlic, crushed**	10	g	1/3	oz
1/4	tsp	**Ginger, minced**	1	g	1/28	oz
2	cups	**Asparagus, cut 1/2" from bottom**	200	g	7	oz
2 1/2	tsp	**Cornstarch, dissolved in:**	6	g	1/4	oz
1/4	cup	**Water**	60	mL	2	fl oz
2	tbsp	**Cooking oil**	30	mL	1	fl oz

1. _Marinate beef sirloin in Mama Sita's Oyster Sauce, 1 tsp garlic, and ginger._

2. _Blanch or steam asparagus. Set aside._

3. _In a wok, heat oil. Sauté garlic. Before garlic turns golden, add beef and stir fry until cooked._

4. _Add asparagus, stir fry to mix thoroughly._

5. _Add cornstarch and water. Simmer for 2 – 3 minutes or until cornstarch is cooked._

CALLOS
(Spicy Casserole of Tripe)

Makes 8 servings.

			Metric		English	
6	cups	*Tuwalya ng baka* (tripe), sliced into 2" lengths	1	Kg	2.2	lbs
1 1/2	cups	*Buntot ng baka* (oxtail), deboned and cut into 2" lengths		1/4 Kg	9	oz
		Water for boiling beef				
3	tbsp	Cooking oil	45	mL	1 1/2	fl oz
2	tsp	Garlic, crushed	6	g	1/4	oz
1	pcs	Onion, minced	60	g	2	oz
1	can	Beef vienna sausage, cut crosswise into 1/4" pieces	226	g	8	oz
1	pcs	*Chorizo de bilbao*, sliced diagonally (optional)	100	g	3 1/2	oz
4	tsp	Tomato paste	16	g	1/2	oz
1	pcs	Green bell pepper, diced	50	g	1 3/4	oz
1	can	Chickpeas	200	g	7	oz
1/2	cup	Potatoes, diced	100	g	3 1/2	oz
1/2	cup	Carrots, diced	100	g	3 1/2	oz
1	pouch	Mama Sita's *Caldereta* (Spicy Sauce) Mix	50	g	1 3/4	oz
2	tsp	Mama Sita's *Achuete* (Annatto) Powder, dissolved in:	6	g	1/4	oz
1	tbsp	Water	15	mL	1/2	fl oz
2	tbsp	Cheese, grated	20	g	3/4	oz

1. *Boil tripe and oxtail in 2 liters of water until tender, leaving about 3 cups broth.*
2. *Heat oil in sauce pot and sauté garlic and onion.*
3. *Add sausage, chorizo, and meat. Stir.*
4. *Add the broth and tomato paste. Bring to a boil.*
5. *Add the vegetables and simmer.*
6. *Add the Mama Sita's Caldereta (Spicy Sauce) Mix and Mama Sita's Achuete (Annatto) Powder. Stir.*
7. *Add grated cheese and simmer until vegetables are done.*

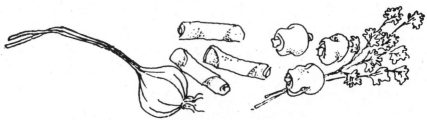

FAJITAS

Makes 6 rolls.

			Metric		English	
Filling:						
1 1/2	cups	**Beef sirloin, cut into strips**	250	g	1	oz
2	tbsp	**Mama Sita's** *Caldereta*				
		(Spicy Sauce) Mix	30	g	1	oz
2	tbsp	**Cooking oil**	30	mL	1	fl oz
3	pcs	**Onions, sliced**	100	g	3 1/2	oz
3/4	cup	**Bell pepper, cut into strips**	115	g	4	oz
2	slices	**Lime juice**				
1/2	tsp	**Salt**	2	g	1/14	oz
1/2	cup	**Sour cream**	113	g	4	oz
Tortilla:						
2	cups	**Flour**	250	g	8 3/4	oz
1	tsp	**Salt**	5	g	1/8	oz
1/4	cup	**Shortening**	35	g	3/4	oz
3/4	cup	**Warm Water**	187	mL	6 1/3	fl oz

For the filling:

1. *Marinate beef in Mama Sita's Caldereta (Spicy Sauce) Mix for 5 minutes.*

2. *In a pan, sauté onion and bell pepper.*

3. *Add the beef and stir-fry. Add salt to taste.*

4. *Remove from the pan. Drizzle the lime juice over it.*

5. *Serve the beef mixture side by side with the flour tortilla and sour cream.*

For the Tortilla:

1. *In a bowl combine flour and salt. Mix well.*

2. *Add the shortening and mix by hand until the dough comes together. Add water and Knead until smooth.*

3. *Divide into 8 equal parts and roll each one into a ball, rest for 30 minutes.*

4. *Preheat oven to 450 °F.*

5. *Roll each ball into 1/8" thick circle approximately 8 inches round.*

6. *Bake for 3 minutes or until tortilla puffs or balloons.*

CHILI CON CARNE
(Spicy Mexican-Style Beef with Beans)

Makes 6-8 servings.

			Metric		English	
1/2	cup	**Red kidney beans**	100	g	3 1/2	oz
2	tbsp	**Cooking oil**	30	mL	1	fl oz
1	pc	**Garlic, minced**	20	g	3/4	oz
1	pc	**Onion, minced**	60	g	2	oz
1	pc	**Red bell pepper, chopped**	50	g	1 3/4	oz
1	tsp	**Salt**	4	g	1/8	oz
3	cups	**Ground beef**	1/2	Kg	1.1	lbs
1	can	**Tomato paste**	227	g	8	oz
1	pouch	**Mama Sita's _Caldereta_ (Spicy Sauce) Mix**	50	g	1 3/4	oz
1 1/2	cups	**Water**	375	mL	12 1/2	fl oz

1. Soak the beans in water overnight. Boil until tender. Set aside.

2. In a heavy skillet, heat oil and sauté garlic, onion, and bell pepper. Add salt.

3. Add the meat and cook until light brown and tender.

4. Stir in beans.

5. Cover and simmer for 10 minutes.

6. Serve hot.

BAKED LECHON

Makes 10 servings.

			Metric		English	
1	Kg	**Pork _kasim_ (shoulder)**	1	Kg	2.2	lbs
1	cup	**Water**	250	mL	8 1/2	fl oz
1	tbsp	**Mama Sita's _Biglang Sinigang_ (Tamarind Paste)**	20	g	3/4	oz
2	pcs	**_Tanglad_ (Lemon grass), pounded**	25	g	1	oz
2	pcs	**_Pandan_ leaves, pounded**	20	g	3/4	oz

1. *In a small sauce pan, combine water, Mama Sita's Biglang Sinigang (Tamarind paste),tanglad, and pandan. Bring to a boil.*

2. *Turn off the heat and allow to cool.*

3. *When cool, remove tanglad and pandan leaves.*

4. *Marinate pork for 30 minutes.*

5. *Preheat oven to 350°F and bake for 2 1/2 hours.*

6. *Increase the heat to 400°F and bake for another 30 minutes.*

7. *Serve with Mama Sita's Sarsa ng Lechon (Sauce for Roasts).*

BREADED PORK CHOP

Makes 5 servings.

			Metric		English	
1/2	Kg	**Pork chop**	1/2	Kg	1.1	lb
1	pouch	**Mama Sita's Breading Mix**	50	g	1 3/4	oz
2	cups	**Cooking oil**	500	mL	1	pint

1. *Rinse pork chop, drain and pat dry.*

2. *Pour Mama Sita's Breading Mix onto a large platter. Roll pork chop pieces and coat evenly with breading mix.*

3. *Heat oil in a medium-sized wok. Add pork chop pieces taking care not to over crowd the wok.*

4. *Fry for 10-15 minutes or until done. Drain and serve with Kim's Sweet Chili Sauce or Mama Sita's Sweet & Sour Sauce Mix.*

Variation: Mix 1 egg with Mama Sita's Breading and pork chop and proceed as above.

CALDERETA
(Spicy Stew)

Makes 10 servings.

			Metric		English	
2	tbsp	**Cooking oil**	30	mL	1	fl oz
1	cup	**Potatoes, cubed**	200	g	7	oz
6	cups	**_Punta y pecho_ (beef brisket), cut into serving pieces**	1	Kg	2.2	lbs
1	cup	**Water**	250	mL	8 1/2	fl oz
1	pouch	**Mama Sita's _Caldereta_ (Spicy Sauce) Mix**	50	g	1 3/4	oz
1	pc	**Red bell pepper, cut into strips**	50	g	1 3/4	oz
1/2	cup	**Green peas**	75	g	2 2/3	oz

1. *Fry potatoes in cooking oil. Drain and set aside.*

2. *Fry beef until slightly brown on both sides. Add water, boil and simmer until tender.*

3. *Add Mama Sita's Caldereta (Spicy Sauce Mix), fried potatoes, and red bell pepper. Cook until the vegetables are tender. Stir once in a while.*

4. *Just before removing from heat, add the green peas.*

Note: *Chicken may be used instead of beef.*

LUMPIANG SHANGHAI
(Chinese Spring Rolls)

Makes 45 pieces. Good for 6-8 servings.

Filling:

			Metric		English	
1 1/2	cups	**Ground pork**	1/4 Kg		9	oz
1/3	cup	***Singkamas* (jicama), chopped** finely	33	g	1 1/8	oz
2	tbsp	**Carrots, chopped finely**	30	g	1	oz
1	pc	**Onion, chopped finely**	60	g	2	oz
1	tbsp	**Mama Sita's Barbecue** **Marinade Mix**	10	g	1/3	oz
1	pc	**Egg, beaten**	60	g	2	oz
1	tsp	**Sesame oil**	5	mL	1/8	fl oz
1/2	tsp	**Salt**	2	g	1/14	oz
2	tbsp	**Cornstarch**	14	g	1/2	oz
2	tbsp	**Cornstarch, mixed with:**	14	g	1/2	oz
1	pc	**Egg, beaten**	60	g	2	oz
15	pcs	***Lumpia* (spring roll) wrappers** (12cm. dm.)(4 3/4" dm.) **Cooking oil for deep frying**				

1. *Combine filling ingredients in a bowl. Mix thoroughly.*

2. *Spoon 1 tbsp of the mixture onto the lumpia wrapper. Roll and seal by brushing the edge with the cornstarch-egg mixture. Repeat process until the filling has been used up.*

3. *Deep fry in preheated 350°F oil until golden, for about 8-10 minutes. Drain off excess oil. Cut each piece into three.*

4. *Serve with Mama Sita's Sweet & Sour Sauce or Kim's Sweet Chili Sauce..*

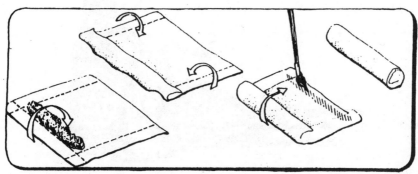

BEEF WITH OYSTER SAUCE

Makes 4 servings.

			Metric		English	
1 1/2	cups	**Beef sirloin, pounded with the back of a knife and cut into strips**	1/4 Kg		9	oz
1	tbsp	**Soy sauce**	15	mL	1/2	fl oz
1	cup	_**Chicharo**_ **(snow peas)**	100	g	3 1/2	oz
2	tbsp	**Cooking oil**	30	mL	1	fl oz
1	tbsp	**Garlic, crushed**	10	g	1/3	oz
1 1/2	tsp	**Ginger, minced**	10	g	1/3	oz
1	pc	**Onion, sliced thinly**	60	g	2	oz
2	tbsp	**Mama Sita's Oyster Sauce**	40	g	1 1/2	oz
1	tsp	**Gin**	5	mL	1/8	fl oz
2	tbsp	**Water**	30	mL	1	fl oz

1. _Marinate beef in soy sauce for about 30 minutes._

2. _Stir-fry chicharo in 1 tbsp cooking oil for at least 1 minute. Remove the cooked chicharo from the pan and set aside._

3. _In the same pan, sauté garlic in the remaining cooking oil until golden brown._

4. _Add the ginger. Stir-fry._

5. _Add the onion and cook until transparent._

6. _Add the beef and cook until slightly brown. Add Mama Sita's Oyster Sauce and gin. If the mixture seems to be sticking to the bottom of the pan, add 2 tbsp (30 mL) water._

7. _Add the reserved chicharo. Stir and serve hot._

VEAL CUTLETS WITH PALABOK PARFUM

Makes 4 servings

			Metric		English	
4	pcs	Veal cutlets, 75 g each	300	g	10 1/2	oz
1/4	tsp	Rock salt	1	g	1/28	oz
1/4	tsp	Black pepper, ground	1	g	1/28	oz
2	tbsp	Coconut oil	30	mL	1	fl oz
4	pcs	*Sibuyas tagalog* (shallots)	40	g	1 1/2	oz
5	tbsp	Double cream or milk	100	g	3 1/2	oz
3	tbsp	Red wine	45	mL	11/2	fl oz
5	tsp	Mama Sita's *Palabok* (Shrimp Gravy) Mix	12	g	1/2	oz

Garnish:

1	cup	Oyster mushrooms, poached	100	g	3 1/2	oz
1	pc	*Calamansi* or lemon, sliced	10	g	1/3	oz
12	pcs	Fresh oregano leaves	25	g	3/4	oz
4	cloves	Garlic, minced	8	g	1/4	oz

1. Season the veal cutlets with salt and pepper. Fry in coconut oil for 10 minutes.
2. Strains off some of the oil then add the shallots. Cook uncovered until brown.
3. Set aside the shallots and the veal cutlets. Keep warm.
4. Mix the double cream, red wine and Mama Sita's Palabok Mix. In the same pan, boil mixture over brisk heat, stirring continuously until smooth and thick. Adjust the seasoning.
5. Pour the sauce over the cutlets. Garnish.

BEEF OR PORK WITH SPINACH

Makes 4 servings.

			Metric		English	
1 1/2	cups	*Lomo* (tenderloin, cut into thin strips)	1/4 Kg	9	oz	
1	tbsp	Mama Sita's Barbecue Marinade	15	mL	1/2	fl oz
2	tbsp	Cooking oil	30	mL	1	fl oz
1/2	pc	Onion, chopped	30	g	1	oz
1/4	cup	Water	62	mL	2	fl oz
1	bundle	Spinach or *kangkong* (Asian watercress)	100	g	3 1/2	oz
1/4	tsp	Black pepper	1	g	1/28	oz
2	tbsp	Cornstarch, dissolved in:	14	g	1/2	oz
1/4	cup	Water	62	g	2	fl oz

1. Marinate meat in Mama Sita's Barbecue Marinade for at least 30 minutes.

2. In a wok or frying pan, heat oil. Sauté onion and beef until slightly brown.

3. Add water and spinach and cook for 3 minutes. Season with black pepper.

4. Pour in the dissolved cornstarch, stirring continuously until sauce thickens.

5. Remove from heat and serve immediately.

Note: Pork or beef tenderloin may be used.

SPICY CALDERETA MEATBALLS
(Spicy Meatball Stew)

This is an interesting recipe, influenced by Western and Asian cultures. It appeals especially to the younger generation.

<u>*Makes 4-6 servings.*</u>

Meatballs:

			Metric		English	
1	tbsp	**Cooking oil**	15	mL	1/2	fl oz
1	pc	**Onion, chopped finely**	60	g	2	oz
1	tbsp	**Garlic, chopped finely**	10	g	1/3	oz
3	cups	**Ground beef**	1/2	Kg	1.1	lbs
1/2	cup	**Bread crumbs**	75	g	2 5/8	oz
1/2	pouch	**Mama Sita's *Caldereta* (Spicy Sauce) Mix**	25	g	1	oz
1	pc	**Egg, slightly beaten**	60	g	2	oz

Sauce:

			Metric		English	
1	tbsp	**Cooking oil**	15	mL	1/2	fl oz
1	tsp	**Garlic, crushed**	3	g	3/28	oz
1	pc	**Onion, chopped**	60	g	2	oz
2	cups	**Water**	500	mL	1	pint
1	can	**Whole tomatoes**	411	g	14 1/2	oz
2	cubes	**Beef bouillon**	22	g	3/4	oz
1/2	pouch	**Mama Sita's *Caldereta* (Spicy Sauce) Mix**	25	g	1	oz
1	cup	**Carrot, diced**	200	g	7	oz
4	stalks	**Celery, diced**	190	g	6 3/4	oz
1	pc	**Green bell pepper, diced**	50	g	1 3/4	oz
4	tbsp	**Spring onions, cut**	8	g	1/4	oz
2	packs	**Flat noodles, cooked**	1/2	Kg	1.1	lbs

1. To make the meatballs, sauté garlic and onions in oil, remove and mix with the rest of the meatball ingredients in a bowl.

2. When well mixed, form into small balls.

3. Heat oil and fry meatballs until slightly brown. Set aside.

4. *To make the sauce, sauté garlic and onions in oil or margarine. Add the rest of the ingredients for the sauce and allow to simmer.*

5. *Add the meatballs gently into the sauce. Bring to a boil, then simmer for 10 minutes. Stir once in a while.*

6. *Add vegetables and cook for another 5 minutes. Serve with flat noodles.*

TOCINO
(Sweet Pork)

Makes 4 servings.

			Metric		English	
3	cups	*Kasim* (Pork shoulder), cut into 1/4" thick slices	1/2 Kg		1.1	lbs
1	pouch	Mama Sita's *Tocino* (Marinating) Mix	75	g	2 2/3	oz

1. *Sprinkle Mama Sita's Tocino (Marinating) Mix evenly over the pork. Knead the meat until its juice comes out.*

2. *When ready to cook, pre-heat a charcoal or gas-fired grill.*

3. *Broil meat one side at a time or cook with 1/2-3/4 cup water in wok. Simmer until the water dries up and fry the pork in its own fat.*

Mama Sita's Instant Pan

sahog Mixes and Sauces

MAMA SITA'S PRODUCTS

Annatto Powder *Achuete*	10 g	0.33	oz
Barbecue Marinade Mix	50 g	1.76	oz
Guava Soup Base Mix *Sinigang sa Bayabas*	40 g	1.4	oz
Marinating Mix *Tocino*	75 g	2.6	oz
Marinating Mix *Tocino*	100 g	3.5	oz
Meat Stew Mix *Menudo/Afritada*	30 g	1.0	oz
Peanut Sauce Mix *Kare-kare*	57 g	2.0	oz
Peanut Sauce Mix *Kare-kare*	100 g	3.5	oz
Savory Sauce Mx *Adobo*	25 g	0.88	oz
Savory Sauce Mx *Adobo*	50 g	1.76	oz
Shrimp Gravy Mix *Palabok*	57 g	2.0	oz
Spicy Sauce Mix *Caldereta*	50 g	1.76	oz
Stew Base Mix *Pang Kare-kare*	50 g	1.76	oz
Stir Fry Mix *Pancit Canton/Chopsuey*	40 g	1.4	oz
Sweet and Sour Mix	57 g	2.0	oz
Tamarind Seasoning Mix *Sinigang sa Sampalo k*	25 g	0.88	oz
Tamarind Seasoning Mix *Sinigang sa Sampalok*	50 g	1.76	oz
Barbecue Marinade	150 mL	5	fl oz
Barbecue Marinade	350 mL	11.8	fl oz
Coconut Nectar Vinegar	355 mL	12	fl oz
Kim's Sweet Chili Sauce	350 mL	11.8	oz
Oyster Sauce	150 mL	5	fl oz
Oyster Sauce	350 mL	11.8	fl oz
Oyster Sauce	680 mL	23	fl oz
Sauce for Roasts - Reg. *Sarsa ng Lechon*	300 mL	11	oz
Sauce for Roasts - Hot *Sarsa ng Lechon*	300 mL	11	oz
Tamarind Paste *Biglang Sinigang*	240 mL	8	oz
Adobo Marinade	150 mL	5.07	fl oz
Adobo Marinade	350 mL	11.83	fl oz
Adobo Marinade	680 mL	23	fl oz
Tapa Marinade	150 mL	5.07	fl oz
Tapa Marinade	350 mL	11.83	fl oz
Tapa Marinade	680 mL	23	fl oz

"A dynasty of five generations of queens of Filipino Gastronomy live today in Manila and have become the ambassadors of Filipino cooking to the world.

The Marigold Commodities Corporation sell Mama Sita's instant food mixes and sauces which go into the pot to capture at once the authentic Filipino taste in your dishes."

Margaret Chan
Wine & Dine - Singapore
August/September 1989

GUIDE TO INSTITUTIONAL USE OF MAMA SITA PRODUCTS
CONVERSION TABLE

A. POWDERED

	Kg./g.	lb./oz.	Equivalent Measure per Pack		Usage
1. ADOBO MIX					
1 pouch (40 pouches =1Kg.)	25 g.	0.88 oz.	3 T +	1/4 tsp.	1/2 Kg. of meat
1 pouch (20 pouches =1Kg.)	50 g.	1.7 oz	1/4 c + 1 T +	1 1/2 tsp.	1 Kg. of meat
1 institutional pack	1 kg.	2.2 lbs.	7 1/2 c + 1 T +	1/2 tsp.	20 Kg. of meat
2. ANNATTO (Achuete)					
1 pouch (100 pouches =1Kg.)	10 g.	0.35 oz.	1 T +	1 1/2 tsp.	11 1/2 cups of rice for Paella
1 institutional pack	1 kg.	2.2 lbs.	9 1/4 c + 2 T		115 cups of rice for Paella
3. BARBECUE MARINADE MIX					
1 pouch (20 pouches =1Kg.)	50 g.	1.7 oz.	1/4 c +	1/4 tsp.	1/2 Kg. of meat
1 institutional pack	1 kg.	2.2 lbs.	5 1/4 c + 2 T +	2 tsp.	10 Kg. of meat
4. CALDERETA MIX					
1 pouch (20 pouches =1Kg.)	50 g.	1.7 oz	1/2 c + 2 T +	1 1/2 tsp.	1 Kg. of meat
1 institutional pack	1 kg.	2.2 lbs.	13 c + 2 T		20 Kg. of meat
5. GUAVA SOUP BASE MIX					
1 pouch (25 pouches =1Kg.)	40 g.	1.4 oz.	1/4 c +	3 1/2 tsp.	1/2 Kg. of fish
1 institutional pack	1 kg.	2.2 lbs.	8 c + 1 T +	1/2 tsp.	12 1/2 Kg. of fish
6. KARE-KARE MIX					
1 pouch (17.5 pouches = 1 Kg.)	57 g.	2.0 oz	1/2 c + 4 T +	1 1/2 tsp.	1/2 Kg. of meat
1 pouch (10 pouches = 1 Kg.)	100 g.	3.5 oz	1 c +	1 1/2 tsp.	1 Kg. of meat
1 institutional pack	1 kg.	2.2 lbs.	19 1/4 c + 1 T +	1 tsp.	10. Kg. of meat
7. MENUDO AFRITADA MIX					
1 pouch (33 pouches = 1 Kg.)	30 g.	1.0 oz	3 T +	1 tsp.	1/2 Kg. of meat
1 institutional pack	1 kg.	2.2 lbs.	6 1/2 c + 2 T +	2 tsp.	16 1/2 Kg. of meat

GUIDE TO INSTITUTIONAL USE OF MAMA SITA PRODUCTS
CONVERSION TABLE

	Kg./g.	lb./oz.	Equivalent Measure per Pack	Usage
8. PALABOK MIX				
1 pouch (17.5 pouches - 1 Kg.)	57 g	2.0 oz.	1/4 c + 2 T + 1 tsp.	1/4 Kg. of rice noodle
1 institutional pack	1 kg.	2.2 lbs.	4 c + 3 T + 2 tsp.	4.1/3 Kg. of rice noodle
9. PANG KARE-KARE MIX				
1 pouch (20 pouches = 1 Kg.)	50 g.	1.7 oz.	1/4 c + 2 T + 1 tsp.	1 Kg. of meat +100g peanuts
1 institutional pack	1 kg.	2.2 lbs.	7 1/2 c + 6 T + 2 tsps.	20 Kg. of meat + 2 Kg. peanuts
10. SINIGANG MIX				
1 pouch (40 pouches = 1Kg.)	25 g.	0.88 oz	2 T + 1 tsp.	1/2 Kg. of meat or fish
1 pouch (20 pouches = 1Kg.)	50 g.	1.7 oz.	1/4 c + 2 tsps.	1 Kg. of meat or fish
1 institutional pack	1 kg.	2.2 lbs.	5 1/2 c + 5 T + 1 tsp.	20 Kg. of meat or fish
11. STIR FRY MIX				
1 pouch (25 pouches =1Kg.)	40 g.	1.4 oz.	3 T + 2 tsp.	1/2 Kg. of assorted vegetables or 230 g. of Canton noodles
1 institutional pack	1 kg.	2.2 lbs.	5 1/2 c + 3 T + 2 tsps.	10 Kg. of assorted vegetables or 2.3Kg.of Canton Noodles
12. SWEET & SOUR MIX				
1 pouch (17.5 pouches = 1 Kg.)	57 g.	2.0 oz.	1/4 c + 2 T	3/4 cup of water or juice
1 institutional pack	1 kg.	2.2 lbs.	4 1/4 c + 3 T + 1 tsp.	9 cups of water or juice
13. TOCINO MIX				
1 pouch (13 pouches = 1 Kg.)	75 g.	2.6 oz.	1/2 c + 1/4 tsp.	1/2 Kg. of meat
1 pouch (10 pouches = 1 Kg.)	100 g.	3.5 oz.	1/2 c + 2 T+ 1 1/2 tsp.	3/4 Kg. of meat
1 institutional pack	1 kg.	2.2 lbs.	6 1/2 c + 1 T+ 1 1/2 tsp.	6 1/2 Kg. of meat